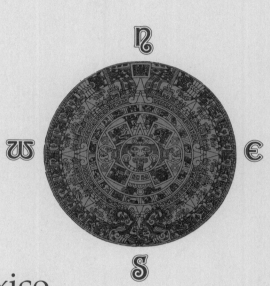

N

W   E

S

Gulf of Mexico

Poza Rica
▲ El Tajin Ruins
etaro

Merida
▲Uxmal
Ruins

Isla Mujeres
Cancun

Campeche

▲Chichen
Itza Ruins

Veracruz

Isla Cozumel

Mexico City
Puebla

Caribbean
Sea

Villahermosa

Jaltipan   Minatitlan

Ruins ▲ Oaxaca
▲ Mitla Ruins

■ Mal Paso Dam

Espero que este
pais sea grande
algun dia y no
mas largo. Jesús

Pictorial Images of Mexico Today

Pictoria

ꟼP **Produced by**

International Pictorial Publications

Created & Directed by William L. Price

Photographed by Jurgis Motiekaitis

Designed by William C. Price

Text by William L. Price

Production by Jerry Jensen

mages of Mexico Today

DEDICATION

The publishers of *Pictorial Images of Mexico Today,* wish to gratefully acknowledge the undaunted effort and invaluable counsel of a man whose confidence in this project has made this literary work a fact. Therefore it is only fitting that *International Pictorial Publications* dedicate this publication to GUILLERMO BRIONES ARAUZ, his country and its people that he lives to serve with invincible patriotic love... the Republic of Mexico.

Produced and published by International Pictorial Publications
49 South Baldwin, Sierra Madre, California 91024
Copyright © 1976 by International Pictorial Publications
All rights reserved, including the right of reproduction in whole or in part
Library of Congress Catalog Card Number 76-405
International Standard Book Number 0-916722-00-7
Printed in the United States. First edition February 1976
Printing and Binding by Graphic Arts Center, Portland, Oregon
Film processed by Olson Photo Associates, Anaheim, California
Typography 10 pt. Optima by Art Page Typesetting, Glendale, California
Covers produced by Smith Pacific Company, Los Angeles, California

CONTENTS

Dear Reader:

On behalf of our country and the Mexican people it is my great pleasure to extend to you a warm welcome to Mexico.

During recent years, there has been a tremendous surge in the development of beautiful and exciting new tourist areas in our country, through the combined efforts of the public and private sectors, which are shown in the pages of this pictorial essay.

New highways, such as the transpeninsular highway in Baja California, have been built to open up previously inaccesible areas of the country, and other areas have been made more accesible through the construction of new international airports and private aircraft landing installations. At the same time, residential and commercial areas, hotels and condominiums have been developed to satisfy the demands of today's most sophisticated tourists.

Thus, places such as Cancún, Zihuatanejo, Rincón de Guayabitos, Manzanillo, San Blas and Puerto Angel are fast becoming as popular as some of Mexico's internationally famous tourist destinations like Acapulco, Mazatlán, Puerto Vallarta, and the Caribbean islands of Cozumel and Isla Mujeres.

Furthermore, we have experienced equally rapid and impressive gains in our technology, industry, agriculture, medicine and the fine arts.

We cordially invite you to visit us and join with us in the enjoyment of our wonderful country.

Sincerely,

MIGUEL ALEMAN

MIGUEL ALEMAN

He served as President of Mexico from 1946 to 1952. He was the second civilian president after Francisco I Madero. As president, Aleman fostered friendship with the United States and encouraged agricultural production. He built hydroelectric plants and irrigation works, and stimulated new industrial developments in petroleum, steel and electric products.

His early professional career was focused on the defense of the interests of miners, railroad workers and workers in the petroleum industry. With this work he obtained a close knowledge with the problems of the working class.

He has been declared, by popular acclaim, in his nation, as the foremost promoter of Mexico.

Pictorial Images of Mexico Today .

. . . is a penetrating new format of photography, text and layout designed to blaze a direct pathway to timely topics pertinent to what's happening now in the Republic of Mexico.

The book contains 320 pages featuring over 400 striking, full color pictures that show facets of Mexico's unique grandeur from magnificent architecture to the latest developments in tourism, ultra modern factories, technology, fine arts, music, cuisine, fashion, scenic beauty, natural history to the greatest of Mexico's resources, her people at work and at leisure.

As a jeweler examining a fine cut precious stone, when you look at the many facets of this pictorial, you will see a kaleidoscopic display of dazzling color pictures and an "up to the minute," informative text. A literary work that will invite you to return again and again to PICTORIAL IMAGES OF MEXICO TODAY for a rewarding experience of rich adventure to be discovered within the magic pages of its artistic splendor.

The publishers have deliberately chosen not to add one more volume to the numerous scholarly volumes already in print about Mexico's rich colorful heritage of ancient Indian civilizations, ruins and cultural blends. Our objective is to expose the world to the evolutionary new Mexico today.

"As Presidente del Consejo Nacional de Turismo," Miguel Aleman stated, "this is the first time that I have agreed to collaborate in the production of a full color pictorial book on Mexico. The project was implemented in cooperative effort with my staff and the William Price Agency for International Pictorial Publications."

The assignment involved traveling 12,000 miles by air and land to the thirty-two states and one district that constitute the Republic of Mexico.

To produce a pictorial on the subject of Mexico is to gather images, literally thousands upon thousands of them, to be edited into a composite that will achieve the objective . . . to answer the question, "What's happening in Mexico today?"

This challenging project began on three islands in the Mexican Caribbean Ocean, just off the tip of the Yucatán Peninsula. Cozumel, Cancún, and Isla Mujeres, adorn the blue of the Caribbean waters with the resplendent beauty of diamonds displayed on a jeweler's velvet. They play a strategic role in Mexico's multi-million dollar tourism development project dedicated to capturing the title of "Tourist Capital of the World."

Speaking of titles, PICTORIAL IMAGES OF MEXICO TODAY, is not designed in the stereotype sequence of theme or topical chapters which contain within each category the sum and total of the message indicated by their headings. We have elected to project a multiplicity of images covering the subjects listed in the "INTRODUCTION" throughout the entire book. For example, one page may focus on tourism and next page fashion. The images on each page contain their own complete message. And yet, as in a mosaic, each piece of tile is necessary to its completeness, so every picture and page makes a vital contribution to the significant composite message of PICTORIAL IMAGES OF MEXICO TODAY.

The preceding pages show COZUMEL, one of the locations included in Mexico's multi-million dollar master plan for the development of tourism. The El Presidente Hotel, located on white sand and limestone beaches, currently has just under one hundred rooms completed with more under construction. The hotel's beach, festooned in a festival of bright colored umbrellas with the background of undulant crystal blue Caribbean waters, is a perfect sublimate for careworn minds and fatigued bodies. The construction boom seen in the picture is symbolic of Mexico's determination to become the *"Tourist Capital of the World."*

Page 11 top — just a few hundred yards away from the hotel on the indulgent coastline of Cozumel is a beach catering to vacationers who enjoy friendly seclusion.

Bottom, a private pool designed to cater to the whimsy of the hotel's guests who prefer tranquil waters to the pounding surf and sand on the beach.

The Yucatán Peninsula, which protrudes up from the southeastern part of the Republic of Mexico toward the tip of Florida, separates the Gulf of Mexico from the Caribbean Sea.

Comprised of three states, Campeche, Yucatán and Quintana Roo, the peninsula is the historic site of a prodigious Maya Civilization. Its name is derived from the Mayan term, "Yuca," thought to refer to the sweet cassava, which resembles the "henequen," a native plant of the region from which the sisal fiber is extracted. The word "tan" means "place of."

Twelve miles off the eastern point of the peninsula, in the state of Quintana Roo, is Cozumel, the idyllic Caribbean Isle. It offers a quiet, slower change of pace for those seeking a place of tropical serenity. Miles of golden sands and palm-lined beaches intersperse bluff coral and limestone shores, set like a precious stone into the multi-layered hues of transparent Caribbean waters which range from the deepest indigo to sparkling topaz and aquamarine.

About twenty-nine miles long and nine miles wide, this low profile island is rich in colorful history. It was visited by Juan de Grijalva in 1518, and by Hernan Cortés the next year. In the following centuries its secluded caves provided hideout retreats for smugglers and pirates. Ruins scattered throughout the jungle, however, indicate the Mayans were there long before, and one theory claims that Cozumel was the motherland of the Maya race.

The stark beauty of the present and faint echoes of the past are the setting for development of Cozumel, Isla Mujeres, and Cancún to be one of the most spectacular and inviting resort areas in the world.

Gustavo Lomelí is rated as one of Mexico's outstanding charter aircraft pilots. He is shown on the wing of Beechcraft's Baron 58 Twin

Right—The aerial view of Cozumel off the left wing tip welcomes Captain Gustavo Lomelí and the International Pictorial Publications team as they make their first landing on the Peninsula.

Mexico's master plan for attracting tourists has not overlooked providing the latest facilities and conveniences for private pilots and charter flights.

Airstrips have been built to cater to the single engine aircraft and small twin engine executive planes. However, Cozumel is a regulation commercial airport where one may see everything from a Piper Cub to a DC 10 taxiing down the runway.

CANCUN is the first fully computerized resort area ever born, and is destined to be the world's number one luxury retreat. In determining the location of the super resort, Mexico turned to the computer, feeding in all of the perfect attributes necessary. Then, corresponding data for various locations in Mexico were fed in and correlated. Cancun was the computer's answer. An island of great natural beauty, it has an average median temperature of 80 degrees and can count on at least two hundred and forty days of full sunshine every year. Warm, crystalline blue Caribbean waters are ideal for skin diving enthusiasts, and water sports of all kinds. Lush jungle vegetation provides a rich colorful backdrop to private lagoons and magnificent ultra-fine sandy beaches.

Following spread —
As you fly over Cancún you see hotels being built, a new jet airport, roads being cut, earth being moved, in total, a complete computer-planned design being carried out in harmony with the island's ecology and surroundings. An entire new society is being constructed from the ground up. Through INFRATUR, a trust to oversee the development, the Mexican government has made an investment of approximately fifty million dollars for the initial infrastructural work. The superstructure of hotels, shopping centers and other facilities are being developed largely by private capital.

ISLA MUJERES, first discovered in 1517 by Francisco de Cordoba, named the island for the many small terra-cotta statues of women he found in its Mayan ruins. Isla Mujeres in Spanish means, "Island of Women."

Mujeres, five miles long and a half mile wide is located six miles off the tip of the Yucatán Peninsula near Cancún. Poised on the point of the island, the Posada del Mar hotel dominates the thatched roof village like a regal queen, providing quality accommodations for those who wish to experience a unique island adventure. Beautiful coral reefs and lagoons exploding with schools of gaudily colored fish make Mujeres a divers delight.

MÉRIDA, state capital of Yucatán, is considered the principal city of the peninsula. It was founded in 1542 on the site of an ancient Mayan city, and today is distinguished for its progressiveness and beauty. Trees with colorful red and yellow blossoms lean gracefully over streets lined with impressive colonial estates of Spanish and Moorish architecture, punctuated by contemporary homes. Below—The circular monument dedicated to Mexico, at the entrance to the "Park of the Americas," is a fascinating sculptured portrayal of Mexican history.

Mérida is the embarkation center for tours to nearby famous Mayan archeological zones. Two of the most notable zones are at Chichén Itzá and Uxmal.

The CORDOMEX, S.A. industrial complex located approximately
10 miles from the capital city of Mérida, is the major manufacturer
of sisal carpets, cloth, rope and twine. Shown on the
preceding page are some of the mammoth machines programmed
to automatically weave innumerable spools of material into colorful
carpets of varied and intricate patterns.

Below—The monument located at the entrance to the Cordomex
factory. The henequen plants, like the one shown here, furnish the
raw material from which all of their products are manufactured.

Next page — Administration building at Cordomex. The landscape
is not only functional but is designed to provide a beautiful, unique
atmosphere for visitors and employees. In the tradition of Mexican
hospitality, Cordomex guests are entertained in an exclusive guest
complex (lower right), complete with pool and recreation
room. The grounds even have a small zoo.

The jaguar, raised by the board chairman's wife as a pet,
had the run of the grounds until he became playfully
dangerous because of his size.

Monuments to a grandeur of the past are often as fascinating and exciting to the tourist as they are to archeologists, who frequently visit the awe inspiring and impressive Mayan ruins of CHICHÉN ITZÁ (preceding page).

Not as large, but perhaps even more dramatic, are the ruins at UXMAL, 50 miles south of Mérida. The beautiful and ornate arches pictured at left are only a part of the Mayan ruins to be found. 118 steep stairs lead to the top of the 100 foot tall Pyramid of the Magician (below), which is actually five temples built one over the other. This is also in Uxmal.

Next page — In another view (top right) of Chichén Itzá, one can see the main pyramid, El Castillo, which is 80 feet high and contains nine terraced bodies with a stairway on each side leading to the summit. The most magnificent remains of Mayan coastal cities is TULUM (below), located on a cliff 40 feet above the Caribbean. It contains 60 well-preserved buildings which provide visitors an interesting journey into their informative and historic past.

CAMPECHE is a blend of the old
and the new. In this picture a
colonial cathedral is seen behind
a new architectural design
located in the plaza. Campeche is
the capital of the state of
Campeche. It is the largest city
between Mérida and
Villahermosa. It was here that
Cortés first set foot on Mexican
soil in the year 1517 and
discovered the Mayan
civilization.

Overleaf, left — Major oil fields
in the state of Tabasco are often in
a rare setting of tropical
vegetation as evidenced in this
site pictured near
VILLAHERMOSA, the state
capital of Tabasco.

Right—This Villahermosa
señorita is an example of
the cultural and ethnic
composite that constitute the
people of Mexico.

The MAL PASO hydroelectric generating station is Mexico's largest and is representative of a progressive future, serving the agricultural and electrical needs of today's Mexico. At present, the plant uses four generators powered by four turbines, and plans call for an expansion to more in the near future.

This important hydroelectric installation dams two large
rivers, the Grijalva and the Usumacinta, which supply
thirty percent of Mexico's water resources. The plant
produces some two and three-quarter billion kilowatt
hours of energy a year, and is the hub of the largest
irrigation system in the country, feeding three quarters of
a million acres. At its highest point, the dam rises some
451 feet.

The PEMEX processing laboratory (left) at the refinery in MINATITLAN is an example of the advanced technology required in this industry today. The oil refineries and pipeline network are comparable to those of the foremost petroleum installations in the world.

An artistic study of industry as seen at the Minatitlán refinery.

39

Pemex (Petroleos Mexicanos) is considered a principal factor in the economic development of Mexico. Petroleum and gas contribute close to 90 percent of the nation's requirements for fuel. Pemex also provides a high proportion of the basic petro-chemicals consumed in agriculture and the manufacture of synthetic products. Refineries are abundant in various areas of Mexico and are typified by the ones in both Minatitlán and Coatzacoalcos, located between Mexico City and Villahermosa on the coast.

Modern gas stations abound throughout Mexico, operated by Pemex (below). Increasing numbers of trained laborers throughout Mexico are being employed and trained by the oil industry.

Pemex is making a significant contribution to a burgeoning army of workers through their training program for the development of skilled industrial laborers.

The Plaza (park) in the center of Mexican towns and cities is a hub of social activities and events in Mexican society.

This colorful Sunday evening scene at Plaza de la Constitución in VERACRUZ, the oldest colonial settlement in Mexico, founded by Hernán Cortés in 1519, portrays the beauty and charm of an important Mexican tradition.

Veracruz is one of the most important sea ports in Mexico, hosting ships from all over the world.

Playing a vital role in the economic growth of the nation is AZUFRERA PANAMERICANA (APSA), the sulphur industry of Mexico. Men working on drilling rigs are an important part of the technique for the extraction of sulphur, which involves the expulsion of liquefied metalloid through use of water injected at high temperatures into the wells.

At the beginning of the twentieth century, many salt mines were discovered, rich in sulphur deposits. However, the depth at which this metalloid was found discouraged its exploitation. The modern technique of water-injection is today utilized universally.

This overview of APSA plant shows the huge storage tanks which contain purified water used in the sulphur drilling operation. Pipes run out of the main plant into vast areas currently being mined. The mining process involves releasing steam from wells which have been injected with high temperature water (below).

Once mined, the sulphur is stored in stockpiles and then loaded by crane onto railroad cars or ships to be distributed to domestic and foreign markets. (Below, right) This APSA worker represents an image of Mexico's invincible bid for a position of industrial power in the international marketplace.

In JALTIPAN the magic of Mexican sulphur processed by APSA has transformed ancient mythology into a modern technology.

From the fire of the volcano came the discovery of sulphur. The contemplation of the volcanos inspired the pre-Hispanic peoples' deification of fire. They attached the magic powers of a personality to a mountain, within which resided Huehuetetl. The most active of these volcanos was named Xitle, meaning umbilicus, because it was believed to be the direct connection to the center of the earth. It was the eruption of this volcano which buried a primitive culture and formed the rocky area on which is now situated the University City of Mexico.

Popocatépetl, the smoking mountain, is second only to the peak of Orizaba and reaches an altitude of 17,887 feet, and along with its snow-capped neighbor, Ixtaccihuatl, has been symbolic of Mexico and guards Mexico City's valley. Before the arrival of the conquistadors, Popocatépetl was visited for purposes of worship to the god of fire, and to gather sulphur from its crater which was used by witch doctors as magical and medical elements in complex therapy.

In 1776, the government established the Royal Gunpowder Factory of Santa Fe, utilizing this sulphur. Fireworks were also produced, which the Mexicans promptly came to enjoy. Sulphur was also used in mining, which had its culmination in the 17th and 18th centuries.

By the 19th century, sulphur quarries were multiplying and the 20th century brought about the foundation of the modern techniques of the Azufrera Panamericana.

In Jaltipan, Veracruz, the main power and heating plants have a capacity of heating over 12 million gallons of water per day to a temperature of 160 degrees centigrade. These installations are designed to operate efficiently 24 hours a day, 365 days a year. The control room of the heating plant is highly automated and the quality of the sulphur is checked by expert personnel. Ample inventory and efficient transportation systems allow the Azufrera Panamericana a displacement of 6,000 tons per day, not only for the domestic market but for export markets.

The major ceremonial city of EL TAJIN is eleven and a half miles south of Poza Rica. It is generally ascribed to the Totonacs or Huastecs and reached its peak around 800 A.D. Typical of the Veracruzan civilization of the Classic Period are the sculptural decorations and the "stepped fret" as dominant motifs (left).

The main structure is the Pyramid of the Niches with 6 terraces, adorned with 365 deeply recessed, corniced square niches that once were painted bright red and blue. The archeological zone (above) covers possibly more than 2,300 acres. Many other structures have been identified but not explored.

The city of eternal lights . . . POZA RICA, in the state of Veracruz, is a city illuminated with voluminous torches ignited by the excess gases from one of Mexico's largest natural gas reservoirs.

Poza Rica, once a village of thatched roofs and dark skies lit only by twinkling stars, has been called by some the land of the "Midnight Flame." The endless burning of the countless torches is responsible for the fanciful title.

It is hoped that the dissipation of energies in this manner will soon be harnessed as productive energy for Mexicans and the industrial furnaces of Mexico.

As for Poza Rica, its rich natural resources have resulted in its transition from a village to a vibrant city of wide boulevards, modern buildings, and prosperity with a promise of limitless and bright economic horizons.

In the picture at the right is a thatched roof hut, a reminder of yesterday, framed in a circle of light from the torch of today.

OAXACA is the principal city of southern Mexico and capital of the state of the same name. In the state of Oaxaca, one of Mexico's most beloved presidents of all time, Benito Juárez, was born of Indian lineage. The 16th century Church of Santo Domingo (left) is a medieval fortress on the outside, while the interior is a startling contrast of ornamentation. The area is famous for its handmade artifacts, including black pottery.

This Oaxacan señorita (left) is wearing a traditional dress of the region. Colorful flowers and handmade pottery are very important to the people here.

The Hotel Victoria is one of the most charming in the city, overlooking the tropical valley from its hilltop vantage point (right). Well-manicured lawns and a sculptured pool sit in a luxuriant setting of palms.

The city of MONTE ALBAN was constructed centuries ago by the Zapotec Indians. It consists of an immense plaza bounded by four large platforms and is situated on a hill overlooking the valley of Oaxaca, five and a half miles southwest of the city of Oaxaca. (Top, far left)

The town of MITLA is twenty four miles southeast of Oaxaca. These ruins (bottom, far left) are located one half mile north of the town plaza. Built by the Zapotecs, the buildings are mud and stone and inlaid with small cut stones. A contrasting image is the Spanish colonial cathedral seen in the background.

Between Oaxaca and Mitla, about a mile off the main road, is a colonial church in a picturesque little village (left).

This giant tree called "EL TULE" (below) stands in the churchyard of the village of Santa Maria del Tule, six miles east of Oaxaca. The tree is estimated to be 2,000 to 3,000 years old, is 165 feet high and 163 feet around its base.

ACAPULCO is more than a vacation wonderland — it is a composite of touristic fantasy. Sun-drenched days spent relaxing on sandy beaches can be interspersed with water sports, some of the best fishing in the world, or just experiencing the flaming sunset over the bay, which dazzles the eye every evening. There's no sun so beautifully tempered with ivory white beaches, balmy climate, cooling breezes and blue Pacific waves as in Acapulco. Acapulco's casual sophistication is surrounded by the uncomplicated and traditional.

Left — The famous Acapulco cliff divers have become a legend. This spectacular dive is from a 136-foot cliff called La Quebrada. In order to perform it successfully, the diver must spring three to four meters out away from the cliff and time the tide just right. The tide must be in, for if it isn't, he will have a very rocky landing.

One of the inspirational landmarks in Acapulco is the white cross with magnificent hands reaching up towards it (right). Located beside a chapel at the summit of the tallest mountain in Acapulco, this steel and granite cross — 150 feet high — is visible all over the bay area. The cross implies that there is something more than jet-setting in Acapulco life.

A panoramic view of Acapulco Bay, whether by day or night, speaks of romance. In the eloquent language of scenic natural beauty by day and, as a wonderland fantasy of multi-colored lights at night, the deep blue bay sparkles like a diamond necklace from over 200 hotels set in a circlet around the shoreline.

63

LAS BRISAS HOTEL in Acapulco is the home of exotic drinks and the cuisine of kings. Pictured above is a creation entitled "The Las Brisas Breeze," filmed amid the ocean spray.

Top right — a cool green thirst-quenching tropical delight. Right — an appetizing selection from the famous buffet luncheon served at the hotel's exclusive La Concha Beach Club.

The preceding pages — For the parched tongue and throat of a desert mirage thirst, a refreshing draught of coconut milk, tapped from nature's tropical keg, is a memorable experience. Or, for the hardier of spirits, this tropical drink made from watermelon will not only lift yours, but accommodate three of your friends as well.

Las Brisas is a most unusual hotel.
Luxurious villas high above the blue sea,
hugging the natural contours of a
flower-banked hillside overlooking
Acapulco Bay. A cascade of pink bungalows
and turquoise pools set on different levels.
All are screened by flowering shrubs and
vines. Every pool is sprinkled with fresh
hibiscus blossoms and is lighted each
evening for a moonlight dip.

The La Concha Beach Club, a palm-lined paradise perched on terraced rocks right over the bay, is one of the most beautiful places in Acapulco. The club is named after the Concha shells found in abundance there.

Assistant manager of the hotel, Pepé Salinas, is extracting the mussel from a La Concha shell, a seafood delicacy that is eaten raw.

A para-sailor approaching a soft landing on the platform. This is a popular sport in the area. The para-sailor is drawn along by a speed boat for an aerial view of the bay and then proceeds to use his own skill and some luck to maneuver in for a successful dry landing.

The Acapulco Cultural and Convention Center is part of Mexico's multi-million dollar plan for tourism. For Acapulco, it's the addition of a new dimension as a convention headquarters. Everything a conventioneer could desire is engineered into 35 acres of colorful flowers and tropical plants at the new Center (right). The facility combines modern architecture with selected reproductions of pre-Columbian archeological pieces to create an interest and appreciation of the ancient cultures of Mexico.

This contemporary sculpture (above) greets visitors in one of the main entrances to the Acapulco Cultural and Convention Center. The structure is nearly three stories high.
A wide variety of events can be staged at the magnificent open air amphitheatre (right), which carries the name of a pre-Columbian king and poet "Netzahualcoyotl." It is designed to accommodate 1,775 people.

ZIHUATANEJO is 154 miles northwest of Acapulco. It has been called the Puerto Vallarta of the future by Mexican developers. Except for the music emanating from the thatched-roof seafood restaurants along the pebbly shore, the only noise is the roar of the surf rushing onto sandy beaches which are partitioned at intervals by rocky, outjutting cliffs.

Water activities, such as skiing, skin diving, snorkeling and fishing abound in this serene resort village. Hunting, horseback riding and putt-putting around the sheltered port in a water taxi to the various beaches are also favorite pastimes.

Emerging out of a virgin section of Mexico's Pacific Coast, some 160 miles northwest of Acapulco, is the biggest industrial project in Mexican history. It is LAS TRUCHAS, a huge steel mill.

The project is in a sparsely populated community west of the Sierra Madre range (rich in iron ore deposits) and bounded by the Pacific Ocean.

The project will impose radical changes on a quiet village people who for centuries have subsisted on fish and coconuts. Almost overnight they will confront a modern urban society with all of its problems and benefits. Developers are keeping priorities in perspective. In addition to building the steel plant, hospitals, schools and other vital systems are under construction for the new Lazaro Cardenas City.

Some $750,000,000 was initially appropriated for the project. Dredging a new harbor to service ore ships from other countries and the installation of a new railway system to Mexico City and other commercial centers will eventually boost the total cost well into the billions of dollars.

More than 15,000 construction workers have been employed in the project which will process ore deposits mined in the state of Michoacan.

Although the plant is situated far from any commercial settlement, it capitalizes on a number of natural resources. These include the rich ore deposits themselves. In addition, the Balsas River, Mexico's largest, is readily accessible and will supply the required power from the new hydroelectric plants. Also nearby is the Acalpican River, on which engineers plan to develop facilities to concentrate ore, which can then be transported overland some sixteen miles to the mill.

The plant is a proud combination of advanced technology, traditional ingenuity and creative exploitation of existing resources.

A ship anchored in the harbor of Las Truchas that transports heavy components to the steel plant and industrially expanding community. Soon, it is planned, the harbor will service big ore ships hauling products from mines all over the world for processing here.

The steel skeleton of the plant which soon will provide steel for construction all over the world rises at Las Truchas.

At right, a center for training skilled employees for the job opportunities presented by the Las Truchas steel mill.

Jalisco, one of the principal industrial states of the Mexican Republic, has more than 450 industries, among which is the wood pulp producing plant in ATENQUIQUE. The plant is nestled in the mountains, and in the background, one can see a dormant volcano, a common sight in Mexico.

A worker shovels one of the products of this wood-pulp producing plant . . . wood chips.

Trucks transport split logs to the plant (above, left) at Atenquique, to be processed. The logs are then run through several chipping machines, brought up by conveyor belts, and the chipped results are stock piled (lower, left).

(above) These children coming home from school happily enjoy their environment.

Housing at special rates (right) is offered as one of the fringe benefits of the company. Employees are also provided schooling for their children, medical care and shopping facilities.

A panoramic view (preceding page) of the beautiful bay of MANZANILLO. As Mexico's major western seaport, Manzanillo is undertaking an extensive waterfront expansion program.

The palatial LAS HADAS hotel, across the bay from Manzanillo, attracts jet-setters from around the world. This resort area has a private marina and a pool the size of a small lagoon, with a unique partially submerged bar where swimmers enjoy a cool refreshing drink without leaving the water.

For the avid golf fan there is a magnificent, private 18-hole golf course to challenge his skill.

Descending from this horsedrawn carriage called "Calandria" is a beautiful señorita. In the background is the Degollado Theater, home of the Guadalajara Symphony Orchestra, the interior of which depicts Dante's Divine Comedy in a neo-classic fresco.

Arches (above) at the entrance of Avenida Juárez greet visitors who will soon pass one of the many monuments, such as the Minerva statue (left), centerpiece of a busy circular intersection.

GUADALAJARA, the incarnate essence of Mexico. A charming blend of the old and the new, the Cathedral of Guadalajara, with its twin 200-foot towers in an unusual architectural mixture of Byzantine, Greek, Gothic and Arabic elements (left) contrasts with the modern structure of the Art Institute (right).

HOSPICIO CABAÑAS orphanage, one of Guadalajara's most noted historical landmarks has been a sanctuary for the orphaned, the widowed, the homeless and the aged for more than a century.

The best known and most dramatic of Orozco's murals, including the world-famous "Four Horsemen of the Apocalypse," line the chapel. Founded in 1801, the structure is remarkable, consisting of 26 flower-filled patios linked by tile passages. A perfect example of neo-classic architecture, it is filled with a great deal of history. It was here that Hidalgo, Mexico's leader of independence, signed his antislavery bill.

Guadalajara is a thriving industrial, commercial and agricultural city; however, it is also known for its beautiful women. Their beauty has become a legend among the Mexicans and the tourists alike. Once again, the enchantment of the old merges with the new in contrast, as evidenced by the differences in dress worn by these señoritas of Guadalajara.

Images of a colonial city, whose streets ring with the music of mariachis and the clatter of horses bearing dashing "charros," are brought to mind by this lovely young lady wearing the classic charro costume, a traditional costume of the past in the state of Jalisco.

"Superior" is one of the famous Mexican beers that is popular nationally as well as internationally. The Moctezuma Brewing Co. of Guadalajara brews a variety of beers ranging from a light, almost clear mixture to a dark brown, heartier drink. Below is Moctezuma's ultra-modern, hygienic brewery.

The automated assembly line (facing page) provides a spotless environment for bottling the beer for a demanding export market as well as local consumption.

The Brewery's complicated piping and filtration system is a study in accomplished industrial design.

Eastman Kodak Co. has established an up-to-date film manufacturing facility in Guadalajara. A technician (upper left) studies color strips to determine the ranges of color film processed. At left, the specialist monitors a machine custom-designed by Mexican engineers to regulate color control. Above, a display of cartridges for use in Kodak's Instamatic cameras. The young man below assembles rolls of finished film just prior to boxing and shipping. Most of the Guadalajara output will be shipped and used within the country.

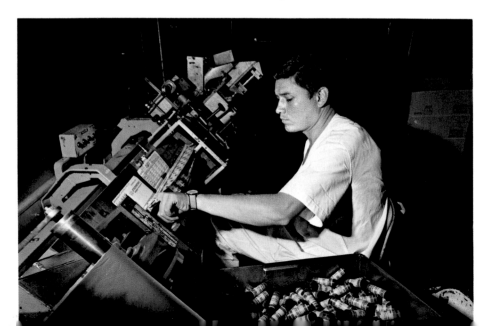

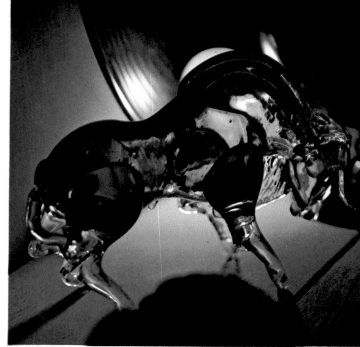

In spite of the economic
attractiveness of mass
production, century-old
processes still beckon
skilled artisans. The
glassblower, framed by a
classic brick archway,
patiently crafts a work of art.

One of the famous glass
bulls is a proud monument
to the patient skills
of its creator.

The artisan, with deliberate
precision, uses a gas torch
to apply the finishing
touches to a sculpture.
While the artistic rewards
are obvious, glass remains
an intricate and exacting
profession for the dedicated
and true artisan.

Left — BARRANCA DE OBLATOS (Monks' Canyon), a few short miles outside of Guadalajara, is a 2,000 foot gorge carved by the Santiago en Verde River. A well-maintained road leads from town to this point, called the Mirador, which features an outdoor theater.

JUANACATLAN FALLS, (below left) one of Mexico's largest, is a pleasant twenty-mile drive from Guadalajara.

Sidewalk vendors artistically carve the common "mango" to resemble a blooming flower. These sprightly bits of color and craftsmanship are a familiar and welcome sight all over Mexico.

LAKE CHAPALA, about thirty miles southeast of Guadalajara, is a favorite vacation spot for "those in the know," the Mexicans, and serves as a retirement haven for Americans and Europeans. This view is of the north shore, near the town of Chapala.

PUERTO VALLARTA, until 20 years ago, was a small fishing village. Today it is ranked as a tourist attraction equal in popularity with cosmopolitan Mexico City and sophisticated Acapulco. Tourists became aware of Puerto Vallarta as a result of the popularity of the film entitled *Night of the Iguana,* starring Richard Burton.

Burton and Elizabeth Taylor have continued to make Puerto Vallarta their second home. Other entertainment people, including rugged director Sam Peckinpah and singer Bob Dylan, have come to Puerto Vallarta on assignment to work and have lingered to savor the beauty and ambiance of this retreat.

Perhaps often missed in the flurry surrounding famous people was the magnetism of the town itself. Jet-setters who literally have the world at their fingertips choose to linger in Puerto Vallarta, and thousands have followed.

The reason is primarily in the incredible beauty of the area. The town lies in the Banderas Bay, where the water is clear and the surf real, and rideable. The huge beach is broken up by dozens of intimate coves. The sand, the surrounding greenery, the sparkling clarity of the blue sky, are the most beautiful in Mexico or the world. The town gives one the feeling of having truly escaped, yet the airport, big enough to handle jumbo jets, keeps civilization, for those who must have it, just a jump away.

Investment and building have transformed parts of the town, promoting growth of condominiums and luxurious houses in the area known as "Gringo Gulch." Other parts of the town retain the charm of cobblestone streets and tile-roofed houses.

Despite the influx of Hollywood and the jet-set crowd, Puerto Vallarta retains its air of intimate seclusion and unspoiled natural beauty, which is why people keep coming.

One may see in the face of this elderly man (reported to be over one hundred years old) a century of quiet and peaceful serenity that pervades the atmosphere of Puerto Vallarta.

A sunset on the beach at Puerto Vallarta elicits a romantic pull on the heart of every person who has ever seen it. Vallarta is one of the few places in the world where palms grow so close to the salt water.

Puerto Vallarta's beach is a collection of dozens of miniature coves, like the one shown below. The irregular coastline provides pleasant accents and surprises all along the way.

Tepic is the heart of a thriving tobacco industry operated by Tabacos Mexicanos, a national trust originally founded by the British-American tobacco syndicate in 1947. The processing plant is the only one of its kind in Mexico, and produces all but about one percent of the tobacco consumed in the country. Thirty-five percent of its output is exported to the U.S., Europe and Japan. Some 5,000 persons are employed in the various phases of production. The government owns 52 per-cent of the plant, which was nationalized in 1972. British, American and other cigarette companies retain a 24 percent interest. The rest is owned by the farmers who grow the product.

This decorative costume is worn with stately dignity and pride by a Huichol Indian, indigenous to the Tepic region.

Bananas, usually associated with smaller countries in the Central American Isthmus, grow in abundance near TEPIC in the state of Nayarit.

MAZATLAN, some 200 miles north of Puerto Vallarta, is a commercial fishing center of Mexico, and a sport fishing center of the world. In the old town square stands its Moorish-style cathedral (right).

Mazatlán supplies over 90 percent of the world's shrimp. Fishing vessels of all kinds, from sport to mass-trawlers to ocean-going refrigerated ships are based here. On the beach, (below) small fishing boats, proudly displaying their names in bold letters, contrast with the sight of a para-sailing enthusiast in the sky above. High rise buildings in the background reflect the image of a booming new industry — tourism.

This seafood platter, (above) as served at Mazatlán's Mamucas Restaurant, is a generous assortment of lobster, crab, shrimp, turtle, swordfish and other varieties, all locally caught. The unique server features its own charcoal brazier, built in, to keep the delicacies piping hot at the table.

Sport fish abound in the waters off Mazatlán. World record trophy fish, including swordfish and marlin, are caught here. At right, the assistant carefully prepares a marlin for the taxidermist, and ultimately for a proud fisherman's home or office.

Canned sardines are part of the rich yield of the waters off Mazatlán, and the canning factories supply an appreciative and demanding export market.

Shrimp are fresh frozen in Mazatlán and shipped to foreign countries, with the bulk going to the United States.

NORMEX brand for sardines joins the
roster of acronyms to name Mexican
national products.

This open country is on the road from Mazatlán, just off the Pacific Coast, heading inland toward Durango. A vista, savage and passionate, yet delicate in its desert-like beauty.

Mexico and leather craftsmanship are often synonymous. Who hasn't seen a picture of a dashing Mexican gentleman mounted on his horse with its ornate saddle and hand-tooled leather tack? LEON, however, known for its leather industry, is catering to the fashion market. The model shown illustrates the high fashion look of today. She wears a flawlessly tailored pantsuit designed and manufactured in Leon.

Calzado Doral, one of Leon's many independent shoe factories, displays some fancy footwork. Most of the well-crafted slip-ons (left) are purchased and worn by nationals.

Worker above skillfully masks shoe soles before the dyeing and painting phase of assembly.

Craftsmen employ modern machines and methods to update the cobblers' art in meeting the challenge of an ever increasing market. Mexicans appreciate the finest materials and workmanship in handsome and durable footwear.

A keen eye and intuitive feel for leather are natural gifts which help the craftsman select the skins used to meet the high product standard of the Emyco Plant in Leon.

On the facing page below, workers in the cutting room prepare the skins according to patterns. Florsheim, a high quality American shoe brand, is manufactured in this plant under the masthead of Florsheim of Mexico. Most of the shoes produced here are for Mexican consumption.

At the right, workers assemble Hush Puppies, a well-known American trademarked brand of casual shoe. Most of these shoes will be shipped to the American marketplace. In the top photo a cobbler operates a machine which stamps soles to uppers. The shoe and sole are then trimmed further and smoothed and, in bottom photo, are sanded and almost ready for shipping.

The road from Leon to GUANAJUATO, capital of the state of the same name, is indicative of the well-maintained highways throughout Mexico. This drive is some five hours from Mexico City.

On the opposite page are two views of the countryside near Guanajuato. The rolling hills at one time yielded rich silver ore, and this hut may have belonged to a prospector. A young boy, below, tends his herd beneath placid skies.

Preceding page: The church of La
Valenciana dominates the hills above
Guanajuato. Still in use, the church is
considered one of the most perfect examples
of colonial building extant. Its delicately
carved facade contrasts with the abandoned
mining structures in the foreground.
These hills once stored a rich deposit of
silver, which resulted in the establishment
of the town.

A painted papiermaché image of Don
Quixote (below) is a popular theme for
artisans throughout the country.

La Parroquia (the parish
church), on the facing page,
is the center of the old
colonial section of
Guanajuato. Inside is the
Virgin of Guanajuato, a
famous image some believe
was crafted in Europe as
early as the seventh century.
It was brought from
Granada in 1557, a gift of
Philip II of Spain.

A modern roof parking
facility in the left foreground
is a striking contrast to
narrow, ancient streets
surrounding the church,
built in 1671.

The Statue of Pipila (left) is dedicated to Juan José Martínez, commemorating the victory of his insurgent forces over Spain in 1830. It overlooks the narrow, picturesque streets of Guanajuato. The car in the center with its headlights on is emerging from the Avenida Subterránea Miguel Hidalgo, an underground street which follows for almost two miles the underground channel of the Guanajuato River, which used to run beneath the city. Some paving on the channel floor and a few lights were all that was needed to convert the channel into a usable roadway. Portions of the city appear above the tunnel exit.

Night photograph of the Avenida Subterránea Miguel Hidalgo shows vehicles traveling through the tunnel, beneath homes perched on the archway. The unique roadway is a busy thoroughfare for incoming traffic only.

124

An ornate exterior distinguishes the TEATRO JUAREZ, facing the plaza of Guanajuato (opposite page). The structure is a combination of classic Greek, Spanish and 19th century romantic.

The distinctive interior of the Juarez Theater is decorated with rich velvet and lined with warm paneling inlaid with intricate hand-crafted design work. It reflects the affluence and pride of its original patrons' Victorian lifestyles.

On the road leading into Guanajuato are two of the most romantic hotels on the continent, the Parador San Javier, in the foreground, and Castillo de Santa Cecilia, just behind it. Both retain the extravagant luxury of another era.

Guanajuato, once a city of silver, is today a city of romance. At right, young lovers share a few tender moments in one of the picturesque plazas.

Below, tables are set for a comfortable open air meal or an intimate tête-à-tête in one of several exquisite plazas which open unexpectedly where narrow streets meet.

On the facing page, two lovers stroll along one of Guanajuato's quaint streets. Many of the streets are so narrow that overhanging balconies almost touch, and a girl living on one side of the street can lean over and kiss her beau in his own home on the other side.

Guanajuato is a city noted for its balconies
and potted flowers. Perhaps nowhere else in
Mexico do the residents love so much to
grow flowers and place them in every
available space.

A motif depicting doves appears and reappears in the silver jewelry around Guanajuato. Local legend has it that the city's first settlers were led there by flocks of doves, long before the fabulous silver strikes turned it into a boom town.

Wearing a shawl of hand-loomed wool, a product of this region, the woman at the right is typical of the varied faces of Mexico. Now in her seventies, she was born a Jamaican and brought to Mexico by her parents at the age of three.

The SALAMANCA refinery of Pemex, the national petroleum trust, is taking on ever-increasing significance because of the worldwide oil shortage. This installation at the city of Salamanca is Mexico's largest, and serves the needs of most of central Mexico. Almost all of its crude oil is piped from the rich Poza Rica fields in the state of Veracruz.

Pemex technicians (below) monitor production in the computerized refinery control room.

The Church of San Francisco in CELAYA is one of the finest monuments to the work of Eduardo Tresguerras, a noted architect and builder of churches. This example of colonial architecture dates to 1629. Its interior is richly appointed, and filled with the results of thousands of man-hours of patient carving and sculpting.

Celaya is the center of a valley called the
Bajío, where most of the colorful serapes,
famous the world over, are woven. The
region is also known for a tasty milk and
sugar candy known as "cajeta."

The valley of Celaya is a rich agricultural region. Framed
by cactus, in the foreground, are rows of staked tomato
plants. This crop is grown primarily for export to the
United States.

Not only is this farmer's machinery modern, but so is his
whole lifestyle. In keeping with a rising trend, he is also
the owner of the acreage he cultivates which includes
the field of tomatoes at left.

At harvest time, workers stream into the fields to pick the rows of plump tomatoes.

Freshly picked tomatoes, still green, are carefully packed for shipment to the United States. They will ripen into a luscious red fruit enroute, and be ready for the table when they reach the stores to the north.

Although modern mechanization, chemicals, fertilization and other advances have lightened the load of the farm worker, some processes must still be done by hand. This includes the picking of produce, such as tomatoes, as it was done generations ago.

Conasupo, a federal agency, functions as an agricultural price stabilizer and farm subsidy authority. They buy directly from the farmer, guaranteeing him a consistent price. Conasupo storage facilities, like these stone bins, can be found all over the Mexican countryside.

Today's farmer is better educated than his forefathers and practices crop rotation and other techniques to coax the most from his land. Knowledge of market conditions is a factor as important as sight and feel in deciding when to harvest citrus trees.

Despite technological advances, the ultimate test is still in the cutting and tasting.

This fine stand of asparagus is no accident. Someday this father may pass ownership of the acreage on to his son and with it, a legacy of patience and judgment.

Two hours northwest of Mexico City is QUERETARO, a city rich in revolutionary history. It is in the process of rebirth as a showcase of industry and planned residential areas.

The town was the last headquarters of the Emperor Maximilian, and it was here that he was executed in 1867.

Here, insurgents plotted their revolutions, and the present Constitution was drafted in 1917.

Pictured on the opposite page is the city's main plaza. The town rests on a valley floor at the base of a long hill called Sangremal.

Outside of the city is an aqueduct, built by the Spanish more than 200 years ago, which is still in use.

The city is the capital of the State of Querétaro.

Just outside Querétaro lies
LAKE JURICA, site of a
planned new residential
development, which
includes a new hotel, the
Hotel Jurica.

This new planned
community is designed
around the historic old
rancho, Hacienda Jurica.

A couple balances along a section of an aqueduct which has been incorporated into the landscaping of the Hotel Jurica.

Another view of the aqueduct, which compliments the beauty of the Hotel's 100,000 square meters of gardens. The structure is functional as well as scenic, supplying a good portion of the community's water.

Guests relax around the Hotel Jurica's pool, just across the lawn from a discotheque.

Below is the hotel's dining room, finished in a rich, traditional mood.

A wrangler bridles one of the gentle but spirited mounts. Guests may ride over the network of trails.

The sun serves up a terrific tan as a tennis enthusiast begins a set on one of the hotel's immaculate courts.

TEQUISQUIAPAN, thirteen miles from the San Juan River, is one of the most impressive communities in Mexico. It is a retreat for well-to-do Mexicans from the big cities, who come to enjoy hot mineral baths.

Preceding pages: Pictured is the archway leading into an expensive residential complex built around a hot mineral pool. On the adjoining page is an example of one of the luxurious homes in the community which, from the outside, looks like just a sleepy village.

Above — Another view of the residential complex, the
pool in the foreground and the entrance archway in the
background.

Pictured at left are the sumptuous interiors of one of the
homes of Tequisquiapan, showing an elegantly
appointed living room and spacious kitchen.

The AVANDARO region, three hours out of Mexico City, is a natural display of verdant greenery, lakes and rugged peaks. This popular resort is also the site of an extensive planned residential development. The view below looks across a fairway of the enticing golf course.

At right is a view from the road into Avándaro, looking over rooftops to the lake. The focal point is a church of contemporary design, presenting an interesting contrast in a land of historic cathedrals.

The pool area of the hotel and golf club in Avándaro is an interesting mixture of design and mood which reflect hints of many cultures. The artistic shaping of the trees, awnings and other vertical structures is almost oriental, while the background is reminiscent of the mountains of Europe.

At right, golfers accept the challenge of the difficult Avándaro links as clouds gather in the sky. After a few scattered showers, they usually disappear as rapidly as they appeared.

The Avándaro's game room of rugged brick and wood is alpine in mood, harmonizing with the nickname of the region, ''Alps of Mexico.'' The golf and country club is the hub of a planned residential development.

On the next spread: The old colonial city of TAXCO as seen in a panoramic view from the veranda of the Holiday Inn. The city's genesis is in mining. Fabulous silver strikes were made in these hills beginning in 1716, and some of the mines are still producing.

Taxco, founded in the colonial days, is famous for its artistry in silver. Above is a tea set which exemplifies the superb craftsmanship of Taxco. In the background are the twin towers of the cathedral, built in 1751, the distinguishing landmark of the region. The twin 130-foot spires were seven years in construction and flank an ornately tiled dome.

Taxco is also noted for its incomparable furniture and cabinet makers.

Intricate carving of tiny objects, such as this crucifix, is another facet of the skills of the Taxco silversmiths.

Weaving by the indigenous Indians has characterized Mexico, and their brilliant, colorful designs are unquestionably identified in the marketplaces.

The Palafox Library, in PUEBLA, two hours east of Mexico City, is one of the oldest in the western hemisphere. It was founded in 1646 by Bishop Juan de Palafox y Mendoza. Today it contains more than 50,000 priceless volumes, many of them hand-lettered by monks. A functional library, not just a showcase, it is used daily by many, including school children.

The courtyard of the Convent of Santa Rosa is an excellent example of the use of Talavera tile, for which Puebla is famed. The tiles have been fired for centuries in the same way, following an ancient Spanish formula.

Puebla is sometimes called "The Rome of Mexico," because of its many beautiful churches. They are so numerous in that region, some say the devout may go to a different church each day of the year. Two examples are the cathedral, above, dominating the central plaza, and the church of San Francisco de Puebla, which freely incorporates local tilework on its exterior.

Pottery and tile are products of the prolific Mexican ceramicists' art. At far left are examples of hand-molded and painted vessels.

Although the volume of ceramic made in Puebla is enormous, virtually all of it is hand done by craftsmen like the potter at left.

Below — An artisan paints the decoration on a large vase. This phase of the production is also done exclusively by hand, before the work is fired and cooled.

The revolutionary industrialization of Mexico has resulted in the dramatic increase of automobiles . . . both on the streets and on the assembly lines. Volkswagen of Mexico maintains a huge plant in Puebla, and other manufacturers, including Ford and Chrysler, have similar plants established in the country. Volkswagen's recent jeep-like model, known as "The Thing," is produced exclusively at Volkswagen of Mexico.

The plant, completed in 1964, manufactures four models on a production schedule of 500 units per day. The factory employs some 10,000 workers with an average payroll of $80,000 a day. The cars are distributed to a network of 146 franchises in the country, and to a large export market.

Below, a front view of the Volkswagen of Mexico plant.

Right, another view of the plant, with a row of "bugs" lined up back to back.

Below right, native shrubbery softly complements the efficiency of the facility.

The automobiles
manufactured in Puebla are
not just assembled here,
but literally built from the
frame up. Here, a highly
complex injection molding
machine fabricates parts
from molten metal.

A worker is shown adjusting a part on a model entitled "The Thing" as it rolls along the assembly line with the familiar "bug" models of Volkswagen.

Stacks of molded fenders are stockpiled, forming an interesting geometric design, awaiting the assembly line. In the background, finishing touches to a VW bus body are meticulously completed by hand.

A trained Mexican welder at work on the assembly line is shown wearing the familiar VW emblem on his coveralls.

Fenders and other parts are painted, then mated with matching color components along the line.

Following spread: Just outside of Puebla, in Cholula, stands the stately Santuario de los Remedios (Sanctuary of the Remedies) Church. Atop a 230-foot hill, the church was built by the Spaniards who aimed to erect a church on the site of each ancient pagan temple they razed. This church was constructed on the ruins of the Tenampa Pyramid, acknowledged as the largest structure in the western hemisphere.

The road between Puebla and Mexico City offers a variety of interesting scenes, harmonizing the old with the new. The bridge in the foreground was built during the reign of Maximilian and is still usable, although the contemporary structure on the new toll road provides a smoother road to travel.

Stalks of corn border a series of villages in the countryside on the way to Mexico City. Ixtaccihuatl, one of the famous twin volcanic peaks, sleeps, massively and silently, in the background.

A panoramic view of MEXICO CITY, the bustling cosmopolitan center of culture, finance and government. The skyline of high rise buildings includes the pointed Latin-American Tower and the striking triangular bank building to its left. This view is from the tallest building in Latin America, the 52-story Hotel de Mexico. In the distance, rugged mountains complete the stunning setting.

The dominant landmark in downtown Mexico City is the Angel, Mexico's monument to independence. Located on the Paseo de la Reforma, the monument is the hub of a traffic circle, one of the city's intersections.

The area occupied by Mexico City is an old lake bed with no underlying bedrock. The combination of unstable subsoil and the basic volcanic nature of the region has made construction of buildings a significant engineering accomplishment.

Left — The 44-story Latin-American Tower was, until recently, the tallest building in Latin America. Of particular interest to structural engineers for its underpinnings, as much as for its visible exterior, the building employs a "floating" foundation over clay.

Right — The 52-story Hotel de Mexico is now the tallest structu in Latin America. Its height and contemporary lines totally dominate the new Mexico City skyline. After seven years of continuous work, the building is soon to be completed

Adjoining the Hotel de Mexico is the SIQUEIROS CULTURAL POLYFORUM, a copious building housing several forums, designed for the development of human communication. Created by famed muralist David Alfaro Siqueiros, the building was six years in construction and murals were painted for the Siqueiros Cultural Polyforum by more than 30 artists from all over the world. The outside of the building is shaped like an enormous 12-faceted diamond, each facet incorporating a separate theme. Inside are immense exhibits: the world's biggest mural, light and sound shows and a host of other artistic and cultural media to please the senses.

The PALACE OF FINE ARTS in Mexico City is the home of the Ballet Folklorico and other important cultural attractions. Built in 1934, the structure initially sunk in the soft soil; this was one of the reasons for the "floating" foundations used in subsequent buildings.

The BASILICA OF GUADALUPE is considered the holiest shrine in Mexico. The church was built here in 1531 after an Indian peasant, Juan Diego, reported he received a vision of the Virgin, who told him that a church should be built on this site. When church officials doubted the Indian's story, the Virgin filled his cloak with fresh roses, and sent him to talk to the Bishop again. When the Indian opened his cloak to show the roses, they were gone, and in their place was a vivid image of the Virgin. Experts from Rome attempted to play devil's advocate and discredit the story, but no suitable explanation for the picture could be found. Today the cloak is encased in glass above the central altar of the church, in plain view.

Another monument to the Virgin is the Chapel of the Little Well. According to the legend, a spring burst forth from the location where the Virgin stood during a vision.

In Mexico City's memorabilia of the past, proud statues
and monuments to the revolution stand in contrast to tall
buildings of contemporary design and structure.
This building is draped with the national colors on
the important holidays.

Another study in contrast is a colonial building seen through ornate ironwork.

In northern Mexico City, just off Reforma Avenue, is a historic architectural showcase illustrating three cultures. In pre-Columbian times the area, known as Tlatelolco, was an important ceremonial site. Later it was the site of the largest market place in Latin America. Bases of pyramids from this epoch comprise a part of the central Plaza. The restored church, dating from 1536, represents the Spanish Colonial influence. The 19-story Department of Foreign Affairs is among the contemporary structures bordering the plaza.

The PETROLEOS MEXICANOS MONUMENT
is a memorial to the oil workers of Mexico
and the nationalization of the
petroleum industry.

Few, if any other, cities in the world have such a spacious, magnificent garden park forest as CHAPULTEPEC PARK located in the heart of Mexico City. It is the home of many museums, such as the Museum of Anthropology, foremost in the world. The park includes recreation facilities, lakes and clear, sparkling fountains springing up in a festival of dancing water, accented by artistry and beautiful sculptures.

View of the city from CHAPULTEPEC CASTLE, a regal building situated on top of a hill about 200 feet high. This was once the palace of the Emperor Maximilian and is now the National Museum of History. Another view of the castle, which after independence was used as the home of Mexican presidents. At one time the Castle was the National Military Academy, and it was here that six young cadets, in the final battle of the Mexican-American War, jumped to their deaths from a parapet, rather than surrender. Statues on the balcony are a memorial to them.

On a pleasant Sunday as many as a half million Mexicans head for the park, a shrine of natural beauty which combines all of the built-in elements necessary for a relaxing and entertaining time for the entire family. The ever present vendors, the balloon man, the cotton candy carts, delight Mexican children who share a sweet tooth with youngsters around the world. Top right — Young men in a challenging foot race. Soccer remains, among sporting events, the favorite game and national pastime.

One of the most ambitious engineering projects of the decade is the vast flood control and sewer project for Mexico City. The system, to be completed at a cost of more than 320 million dollars, features two huge tunnels, 15½ and 16½ miles long, and a 31-mile outfall tunnel. The system replaces the city's Grand Canal, in use since the turn of the century when the city's population numbered only a half million, compared to today's 10 million-plus. The new system is designed for a population of 26 million.

Above — Hydraulic and structural engineers confer at the project.

Left — A welder creates his own eerie sun deep in the recesses of a tunnel.

Top right — Workmen apply finishing touches to the huge storm drain. During the rainy season this cavern will be completely filled with rushing water.

Right — The storm channel exits above ground and the water continues to be carried via aqueduct.

189

The National Housing
Institute Fund directs the
program for upgrading
housing for low income
workers. The capital is
contributed by private
enterprise and the federal
government. This objective
is achieved on two levels:
first in refurbishing
present dwellings of
workers, secondly through
vigorous new construction
of housing developed for
the lower and middle
income strata.

The top picture is an
example of a middle class
development in Mexico
City. The next picture
shows a suburban dwelling,
and, at bottom, is a typical
street scene in a modern
middle-income
neighborhood.

Handsome housing developments in conjunction with beach clubs, tennis or golf clubs are increasingly changing the Mexican living profile.

This unique Las Gaviotas Beach Club is on Descanso Bay in Baja, California, 30 miles from the U.S.-Mexican border at San Diego and Tijuana. With the beach club as their hub, new houses and condominiums are being completed daily.

Commuting in Mexico City is no problem for the visitor or resident because of the variety of efficient public transportation systems. A fleet of modern buses services major points on precise and regular schedules. The Metro system, among the most modern in the world, is highly efficient and inexpensive to ride. Mexico City planners have solved the complex problem of building these systems in a city with a large and spread out population. Rapid transit experts from such cities as Los Angeles have watched with envy as the system has grown. For those who prefer, there are Mexico City's taxis, with good drivers adept at getting from one point to another in the least possible time.

Mexico's City's department stores, specialty shops, boutiques and large malls are as modern, luxurious and varied as any in the world. From the chic Zona Rosa area downtown to the Satellite Center, Mexico City is a shopper's dream. The striking chandelier at left is in the El Puerto de Liverpool department store in the Satellite Center Mall. Above and below are windows of other stores in the Mall, reflecting elegance on a par with any in the world.

A tempting array of merchandise for the shopper is offered in the ZONA ROSA, or Pink Zone, a sophisticated business and shopping center downtown. The boutique at right beckons with native costumes, primarily for sale to the visitor.

Fish, lobster and wine on ice stimulate the appetite at a gourmet shop.

An example of the fine silver and jewelry available in many of the exclusive shops of the Zona Rosa.

Reflections of a passing
scene in the Pink Zone.

A sidewalk cafe extends an
invitation to sip an aperitif
and relax in the
cosmopolitan ambience
of the district.

Famous labels from all over
the world are represented in
this shopper's paradise.

The creativity of Mexican
designers is exhibited in
these gowns. The dress at
left features embroidered
accents with a traditional
touch. The spicy red
ensemble makes a more
daring statement while
retaining the traditional
Latin mood. Both gowns are
designer high-fashion, and
are not necessarily
representative of what the
average Mexico City
woman might choose
for herself.

In a country where flowers bloom perennially and flower markets are as numerous as rosebuds in a rose garden, it is only reasonable that the prolific aromatic blossoms of beauty and exciting color are as much a part of the Mexican's daily life as his food and music. Flowers grace the home, the office, and even the person. They are found in vases in automobiles and tied precariously to motorcycles. In Mexico, flowers are everywhere.

Left — A brilliant hibiscus blossom.

Right — Scenes at a typical open air flower market.

Just as the sacred music of the Mass is part of the worship, and not just a diversion or background, so is the music of the mariachis an integral part of the Mexican's existence. In Mexico, "mariachis" play when a baby is born, when he grows up and courts his first sweetheart, at his wedding, and even at his funeral. Here, these "marimba" players are a part of the regular BAZAR SABADO, a large gathering each Saturday on the grounds of a former convent where Mexicans come to shop and barter and visit.

Top right — A pineapple festooned with olives, shrimp and other succulents.

Above — An appetizing procession of traditional Mexican dishes, prepared and served by a charming señorita in the courtyard of the Bazar Sábado.

Right — Fruits and melons are prepared in a cluster arrangement decorating a bubbling fountain with the same artistic skill of a florist preparing a stunning floral piece.

Some of the most talented and sophisticated artisans and craftsmen in Mexico make one of their headquarters . . . the Bazar Sábado. Located in San Angel, on the southern edge of the city, the area is a favorite haunt of the more successful artists.

Fine sculptures, colorful tapestries and handicrafts of all types are displayed at the Saturday bazaar.

Copper and woven wicker are among the popular handicrafts available at Bazar Sábado.

The courtyard of the SAN ANGEL INN is part of a carefully restored 18th century hacienda.

The inn features gourmet cuisine and has won international awards from noted critics. It is, indisputably, one of the great restaurants of the world.

Interior of the Inn, with the lavish buffet table set for luncheon.

Drinks as pictured here are prepared and served at the San Angel Inn with the same care and inspiration as their cuisine. Experts recommend the superb margarita, and give highest marks to their martinis.

The colossal umbrella, half the size of a city block, covering the interior patio of the MUSEUM OF ANTHROPOLOGY in Mexico City, is internationally recognized as an architectural and engineering masterpiece. Designed by Pedro Ramírez Vásquez, recognized internationally as one of the foremost architects, the whole structure is supported by a single pillar, 40 feet high, and artistically sculptured in bronze.

Suspending this tremendous structure by one single pillar was a challenging problem in its own, but the additional complication of constructing it on the unpredictable soil strata of Mexico City makes it an impossible dream come true. Constructed in 1964, the umbrella has stood the test of numerous earthquakes in Mexico City.

PEDRO RAMIREZ VASQUEZ, architect and designer of Mexico City's Museum of Anthropology, is a dynamic example of Mexico's rich human resources. His projects, specifically in Mexico City . . . each one a significant landmark . . . are a triumph of engineering and a monument to his architectural genius. These structures include the Exterior Relations Building, Plaza of the Three Cultures, Modern Art Museum, Aztec Stadium, Ministry of Public Works, Japanese Embassy and the new Basílica of Guadalupe.

Among his foreign assignments are the Center of Exterior Commerce in Marseilles, France; a museum in Senegal, Africa; the new capital of Tanzania; the Museum of Tehran, Iran; and he is also consulting in the planning of Jerusalem in Israel.

Following spread — Entrance to the Museum of Anthropology.

On preceding page — Entrance to the Museum of Anthropology in Mexico City.

The Museum of Anthropology is universally recognized as one of the finest museums in the world. Constructed around a 600-foot long central patio, it contains individual sections devoted to the ancient civilizations of the Republic. It is designed to involve the visitor in an atmosphere of participation with the archeologists who unearthed the historic artifacts and to present them with the wonder and dignity of the great civilizations they represent.

Some of the most interesting exhibits are those of relics excavated during the building of Mexico City. One of the dominant artifacts in the Grand Exhibition room is, Coyolxauhqui, (pictured to the left) a 1,543 pound Aztec moon goddess of jadeite, whose grinning face and half moon shaped eyes are fringed with golden rattlesnakes.

Pictured on the following page is the main exhibition room located at the far end of the central patio. As the most popular single treasure unearthed in any country in the western hemisphere, the Aztec Calendar Stone (background) is given the place of honor. In the foreground, is "She of Serpent Skirt," the Aztec name for the grisly Coatlicue, mother of dieties. Her decapitated body sprouts two serpents, symbols of blood. Her necklace links human hearts and skulls. First unearthed in Mexico City in 1790, she was quickly reburied by a Spanish priest to discourage her worship.

At left — A spectacular mural and carvings in the exhibit room, just before entering the Tomb of Palenque. Discovered in a tropical region of the state of Chiapas, it is one of the most unique displays in any museum in the world. The visitor descends steps, into the exhibit as if he were entering the tomb at the actual archeological site.

Right — Bones are displayed exactly as they were found.

Below — A replica of the burial vault.

Bottom Right — A jade death mask, actually placed over the face of the fallen prince found in the tomb.

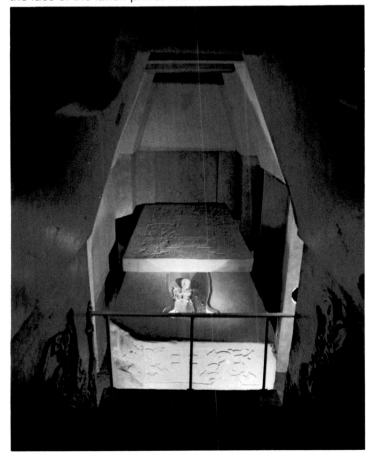

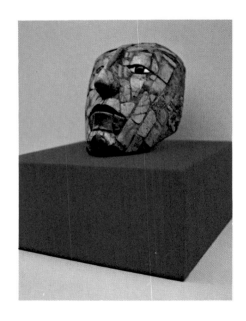

216

The beautiful, modern architecture of the Albatros School in Mexico City is indicative of the importance Mexico places on education. The curricula offered here include the elementary grade levels through a challenging and progressive college preparation program.

Classrooms are designed to provide a pleasant and conducive atmosphere for learning.

The recreational field, shown, is consistent with the importance placed on physical fitness as a necessary element for developing a well-balanced individual.

UNIVERSITY CITY, also known as the National University of Mexico, is one of the oldest universities in the western hemisphere. Founded in 1553 by special charter from the King of Spain, and known then as the Royal and Pontifical University of Mexico, it was closed about the middle of the 19th century to be replaced some 60 years later by today's institution. At that time, its colleges were scattered throughout downtown Mexico City. However, during Miguel Alemán's presidency, around 1950, University City was started and completed in a record four years.

The campus is growing every day. Currently, it occupies 1,500 acres and accommodates over 30,000 students. From its beginning in 1921, the National University of Mexico was the first in Latin America to offer summer school courses for foreign students. The school for foreigners has now grown to an intensive all-year program.

Some of the most famous artists in Mexico have contributed to the vast amount of murals, mosaics and statues that make up this artistically and architecturally striking campus.

Juan O'Gorman, one of Mexico's most famous artists, covered all four sides of the ten story Central Library with an incredibly intricate and beautiful mosaic mural depicting the history of Mexico from pre-Columbian times (preceding page). The administration building (right) is another example of the mixture of the old and the new, with its modern architecture and colorful mosaic. The theme of this institute of higher education is appropriately depicted in another of its murals: "The people go to the university, and the university goes to the people."

The School of Medicine building at the
University displays Eppens Helguera's
mosaic mural "Life and Death," which
symbolizes birth of the Mestizo, the Mexican
derived from Spanish and Indian ancestry.

Inside the University of Mexico are the latest facilities for the most sophisticated pursuit of academic disciplines.

A typical classroom situation is pictured at the top. Also shown is a laboratory facility in the medical school and, below, engineering students perform experiments in water purification research.

The Atomic plant which serves as both a center for nuclear research and the processing of isotopes is located just outside Mexico City. Modern architecture is combined with colorful mosaics in the administration building of the center.

In a setting of scenic hills surrounding Mexico City, the plant blends in with the countryside.

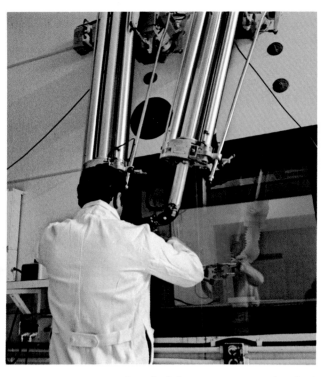

A technician operates mechanical equipment which allows him to handle hot isotopes from behind a protective safety barrier.

The unpretentious tank structure housing the nuclear reactor as viewed from below does not betray the dramatic scientific potentials it confines.

When viewed from above, one can readily see the purple glow of the nuclear reactor when it is activated.

Pictured above — The NATIONAL MEDICAL
CENTER of the MEXICAN INSTITUTE OF SOCIAL
SERVICES is one of many in the network of medical
facilities that supply Mexico City with some of the
finest health care in the world.

The latest medical equipment and skilled technicians are required in the practice of diagnostic medicine and medical research.

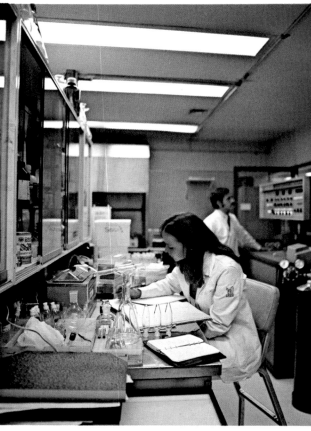

Pictured are some of the eminent doctors of
Mexico City. From left to right, Dr. Emilio Exaire
F.A.C.P., professor and chairman of the department
of Nephrology; Dr. Masao Kume, assistant
professor of Otolaryngology; Dr. Gregorio Mintz
F.A.C.P., professor and chairman of the department of Rheumatology; Dr. Jorge Corvera,
professor chairman of the department of
Otolaryngology; Dr. Juan Alberto Sanen Ahued,
specialist in Neuropsychiatry; Dr. Enrique
Cárdenas De La Peña, assistant to the subdirector
general of the Mexican Institute of Social Services.

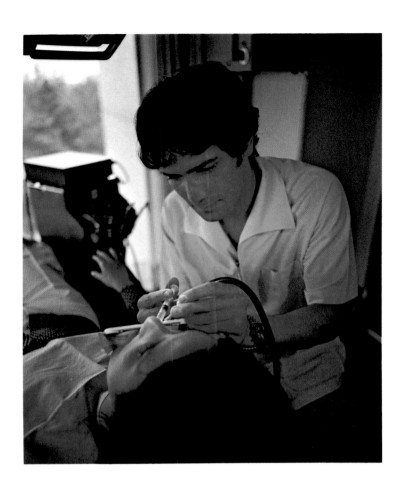

DR. CARLOS E. KOLOFFON, brilliant 29-year-old oral surgeon and specialist in edodontics, studied in Mexico City, and completed postgraduate work at Baylor University and at the Philadelphia Dental Society. Dr. Koloffon has written numerous articles for international professional journals. He is noted for his work in pioneering and refining techniques for performing oral surgery using a "rubber dam" process to insure a sterile isolation.

Dr. Koloffon shown employing his simplified rubber dam technique during a root canal operation. His office in Mexico City is a showcase of the latest dentistry equipment available to the profession.

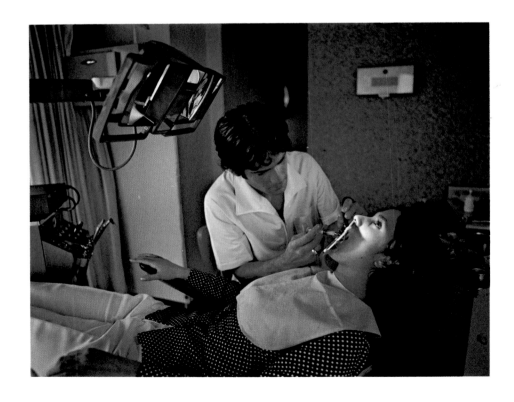

DR. OSCAR FARIAS, Mexico's internationally known hearing specialist, is considered a Mexican pioneer in the rehabilitation of the deaf. Dr. Farías was the youngest of three founding directors of the National Institute of Human Communication in Mexico. As past general director, and currently as a special advisor to this government institute, he has made giant strides in developing modern rehabilitation techniques which teach the deaf to communicate more normally and thus become a useful part of society.

Today, the majority of Dr. Farías' time is spent, however, in the treatment and research of very young children, classified as totally deaf, at the private clinic called OIRA (Infantile Orientation and Rehabilitation for Hearing). OIRA, which in Spanish means "He will hear," was co-founded in 1962 by Dr. Farías and a patron, Mrs. Enalda Luttman, who became involved because her son suffered a hearing disorder.

Dr. Farías believes that virtually all youngsters classified as "deaf" from birth, actually have some form of residual hearing that can be cultivated, but often lose the ability to recognize and link it to meaningful communication. He feels children must begin with hearing aids and other treatment very young, preferably as infants, before they begin to adjust and over-compensate for their handicap. With proper early diagnosis, amplifying sounds, and stimulating the latent sense of hearing, he is convinced that most of these youngsters can be rehabilitated. Another important thrust of his treatment is in re-orienting the afflicted persons and those around them who are locked into a preconditioned view of the person as deaf. If deaf people are treated as hearing persons, they will tend to communicate as do hearing persons, relying less on sign language and other aural "crutches."

The doctor's therapy, then, consists of six steps: adaptation of hearing aids; early audio training; structuring of speech through the child's natural faculties (as opposed to sign language, etc.); rehabilitation and development of the child's psychosomatic adaptation (thinking and acting as a hearing person); cooperation of the family within the rehabilitation plan; incorporation of the child into normal family, pre-school and regular social activities.

Right — Dr. Farías with young patients at the National Institute of Human Communication in Mexico City.

Above, a trained OIRA therapist-teacher works with a young deaf boy, teaching him to link the amplified sounds or vibrations he is sensing into specific actions. His mother, who is looking on, must also be involved in the therapy and training process to learn to treat her son as a hearing person. At the left, Dr. Farías discusses genetic factors that affect hearing disorders with laboratory technicians.

With the patient, skillful use of this hearing aid at OIRA . . . the light of understanding glimmers in the eyes of this young boy . . . and he is able to link the sensations of sound to the actions communicated to him by his teacher.

Ultimately, he will develop the ability to live and communicate in a normal manner, not relying on sign language or any other aural "crutches."

The Sports Arena, also known as the Palacio de Los
Deportes, was selected as the location for the historic
first national industrial exposition in Mexico City.
Everything from kitchenware to heavy equipment was
displayed, illustrating the acceleration of Mexican
industrialization.

A view of a typical booth at the industrial exposition shows modern chrome furniture being displayed. Briones S.A., founded in 1934, was the first chrome furniture factory established in the Republic of Mexico.

Guillermo Briones Arauz is President of Briones, S.A., President of BrioTubo, S.A., Vice President of Briones Real Estate, S.A., and Vice President of the Consulting Committee for the National Association of Importers and Exporters of the Republic of Mexico. For over forty years he has served his country as a confidant to the Republic of Mexico's succession of Presidents, specifically, in the sciences of world trade and industrial technology. His personal success has proven that with vision and indefatigable work the people of a nation will prosper. Furthermore, they shall fulfill their individual responsibility for posterity in contributing to the development of a strong, enduring national economy. Guillermo Briones is the recipient of the subsequent decorations and commendations: March 4, 1971, Decorated by His Majesty King Bandowin of Belgium as "Gentleman Of The Order Of The Crown"; March 11, 1971, Awarded the "Foreign Trade Medal Of Merit" by the National Association of Importers and Exporters of the Republic of Mexico; September 6, 1971, honored and conferred in Naples, Italy, the title of "Commendable of the Military Order of San Salvador, and Santa Brigida of Switzerland."

Right — Guillermo Briones Arauz . . . discusses with his foreman the results of a test run on metal plates at the new laminating plant located just outside Mexico City. Metal plates are components in the manufacturing of Bromica (Formica).

Pictured below is a department of the Briones, S.A. Factory founded by Guillermo and Carlos Briones. This department is the upholstering division.

Carlos Briones Arauz is the engineering genius behind the great number of Briones manufacturing enterprises. He is the recipient of many honors in the technological disciplines of industry. Carlos has also taken time to champion, with his leadership, a multitude of humanitarian causes within the structure of the Rotary Club. As his own individual project he designed, funded and developed a prospering model Indian community.

Pictured to the right is a — *Swiss plywood press* — located in a section of the astonishing new laminating factory, labeled currently as the most sophisticated laminating installation on the North American continent. The factory has over 52,000 electrical connections and 52 kilometers of electrical cable running to monolith presses, control panels and equipment. The production capabilities are rated almost unlimited and the factory is designed to be operated by fifty technicians.

To the left is a view of a department of the BrioTubo Factory where pipe is stored, cut and shaped into the frames and foundations used in the designs of "prize winning" chrome furniture for homes, offices, hotels and wherever furniture is used in Mexico. The American Electro Fusion machine shown is used in the manufacturing of cold roll automotive parts: drive shafts, axles and axle housings.

Following spread — A surrealistic image of the mood, color and excitement of the Ballet Folklorico.

237

The Ballet Folklorico of Mexico is a splendid pageant of disciplined dancers developed and trained in the rigorous traditions of classic ballet, performing the liveliest and most romantic Mexican music, and colorful dancing. Stunning costumes and scenery create exciting settings and mood transitions from the ancient civilizations to modern Mexico.

The company was organized in 1952 by Amalia Hernández. Trained as a classical ballerina, she felt unfulfilled by established dance. Then, virtually in her own backyard, she discovered in the history and tradition of Mexico, a vital, untapped reservoir of spectacular ballet. From this source she created choreography rooted in the passion and fire of Mexican legend, history and literature, weaving this into what is now internationally recognized as a Mexican cultural classic. There are now two companies, a national company performing regularly in Mexico City and a touring aggregation.

Left from top to bottom — The Ballet of the Revolution is one of the favorites performed by the famous Ballet Folklorico de Mexico company and perhaps one of the most relevant in these times. It is dedicated to the "Soldaderas," women who fought side-by-side with the men in the Revolution of 1910.

The Jalisco Ballet opens with a mariachi parade playing lively songs at the start of a fiesta. During the fiesta, the dances, "El Tren," "El Tranchete," "La Negra" and "El Jarabe Tapatío" (the famous "Mexican Hat Dance") are performed. At the end of the performance, the dancers salute the audience, throwing colorful paper streamers to them.

The Veracruz Ballet begins with a haunting "Jarocho Lament," inspired by the human suffering of those who were transported to Veracruz on slave ships from Africa. In contrast, the lament ends with a wave of spirited songs played by a typical Veracruz band. The ballet ends with the traditional "La Bamba," in which a dancing couple ties a large ribbon into a bow with their feet.

Right — Singer in the ballet of the Revolution waits off stage ready to go on.

In a rare departure from the custom of the ballet company, a premier dancer consented to pose in one of the white dresses from the Veracruz Ballet in this outdoor setting.

In much of the repertoire of the Folklorico, women are portrayed as proud, energetic and strong. The face of this ballerina mirrors the fire and pride of the Mexican tradition.

The surroundings enhance the color and beauty of the costume from the Jalisco Ballet, displayed gracefully by the Folklorico ballerina.

The "charreada," the counterpart of the Wild West Rodeo, with all of its excitement, competition and colorful action, tests to the limit the equestrian skill of the "charro." A source of pride to the "charro" is that the utilitarian use of the lariat on cattle ranches has progressed in popularity to a status of an exciting sport.

The Mexican male equates his masculinity with a desire to be utterly virile. His goal is to be forceful, brave, aggressive and scornful of danger and death.

The "charro" (left) must keep on his huge sombrero through all of the strenuous activities for, if he loses it, he will lose points on his final score.

Symbolic of the "charro" are these leather gloves, the lariat and the ever present sombrero (below).

A young, aspiring "charro" looks forward to his first round in the ring. One of the events he will participate in, called "coleada," brings steers thundering out of their pens. The "charro" must then grab the steer's tail at full gallop, twist it around his leg, increase the speed of his mount and flip the animal over on its back into a complete roll.

An image of the past and the present is seen in the visage of this seasoned "charro." The mustache is a symbol of force, power and masculinity. The years of time and experience have etched their lines into his face, which with a bit of imagination can be retraced . . . as a roadmap . . . back through exciting, fulfilling experiences of his youth.

Men of all walks of life are seen participating
in the "charreada." They come to display their
skills in roping and riding.

Mexico has not escaped the enthusiasm for the ever popular body conditioning sport of tennis. Regulation courts have been built in beautiful scenic settings easily accessible for use by the nationals and visitors to Mexico. The tennis equipment available is second to none.

One of the showplaces of Mexico is the HIPODROMO DE LAS AMERICAS, five miles from downtown Mexico City, which hosts horse racing three days a week, year 'round. While the nationals who attend frequently and in large numbers pay regular admission, tourists pay only the tax fee on the inexpensive ticket.

Rounding the stretch, this jockey is most likely unaware of the crowd that has turned out to witness and bet on his success (left).

As the horses approach the finish line, they pass the modern tote board at the Hipódromo.

Mexico has achieved world prominence in Olympic track and field events, in baseball and, recently, in the Davis Cup and other international tennis events. Soccer, however, is played the length and breadth of the country, in open fields, country lanes and parks, by children, by young adults and by professionals. Its universal acceptance and popularity has prompted some to classify soccer as a national sport.

At left is the Aztec Stadium in Mexico City where large, enthusiastic crowds turn out regularly for a giant, unending "Super Bowl" of soccer.

At right, young men hone their skills, many with the dream of someday being a professional soccer hero.

Carlos Esteva conducts a string ensemble of young men in a concert at a popular resort town near Mexico City. Differences in social and ethnic backgrounds are knit together into a harmonious musical unit under Carlos Esteva's patient direction.

CARLOS ESTEVA, noted Mexican concert violinist, is the founder and director of the Classic Orchestra of Mexico. Esteva is dedicated to the promotion of performances of orchestral chamber music and to stimulating a base of broad Mexican interest in this field of musical activity. He has created a "Children's Orchestra" and the "Juvenile Chamber Orchestra," known as the amateur section of the "Classical Orchestra of Mexico," which is a practical workshop for the development of music students. Here, they learn to play in orchestral groups and are prepared to integrate any professional chamber orchestra.

The Carlos Esteva quartet is a professional
string quartet which travels throughout
Mexico, playing classic chamber
music in concert.

Prominent in Mexican classical music circles, and a favorite of European audiences, is Mexican concert cellist GILBERTO MUNGUIA. A critic in a Copenhagen newspaper wrote: "His Mexican temperament breaks out when he absorbs himself in his instrument. It is only justice to say that Gilberto Munguía has more than temperament. He also has a solid technical skill, a beautiful tone, and a fine sense of bowing. Here was combined liberty and fire in the expression, with deep absorption in the peculiarity of the music."

Mexico is an art lover's paradise.
Some of the most famous water color artists in Mexico are gathered
on a sunny Saturday afternoon at the San Angel home of Licenciado
Eduardo Delmar and his lovely wife, to compare techniques and
create in an atmosphere of comradery. In the picture above,
Licenciado Delmar, kneeling down in a white coat, is the newest
member of this famous water-colorist fraternity. He is discussing a
painting with the artist, Joaquin Martínez Navarrete, known as ''the
painter of the City of Mexico.'' His water color paintings of
famous buildings and plazas are considered incomparable.

Right — General Ignacio Beteta . . . the master water color painter of landscape is of international fame, identified especially for capturing the rich flavor of Mexican atmosphere. The General served as a soldier in the 1910 revolution and is currently an active General of the Mexican Army. He, himself, personifies an artistic study of the color of Mexico.

Below — In the foreground, artist, Fernando Casas applies finishing touches to a new work of art. Fernando is considered the romantic of the group and is well known in the United States for his "Tiánguis," (Mexican typical market scenes) and for his technique of using soft colors. In the background, Eduardo Delmar, increasingly renowned as an outstanding water-colorist in his own right, discusses his artistic approach with Rafael Muñóz López. Licenciado (lawyer) Delmar paints from what his imagination or "inner mind" sees, rather than from a world of realism. His works are an exciting display of color and ethereal design.

Right — Rafael Muñóz López, considered by his peers as the best water-colorist in the world for painting human figures and portraiture.

The city where the meaning of contrast is changed to blend: the old and the new, languages, races, color, all become a charming singular unit expressed in two words, Mexico City. As night falls, the Paseo de la Reforma illuminates its skyline and turns it into one of the brightest cities in the world. (opposite page)

In an older, colonial section of the city (above), cobblestones wind their way in a more traditional manner.

The CATHEDRAL OF MEXICO, one of the oldest and largest churches in the western hemisphere, was constructed on the site of an ancient Aztec temple, in 1567. The facade is highly ornamented limestone, a mixture of Doric, Ionic and Corinthian architecture. Highlighted on the outside by the twin bell towers which rise two hundred feet above the street, the interior contains many beautiful paintings, carvings, marble statues, and chapels.

The Cathedral faces the immense Plaza de la Constitución, called the Zócalo, which is the political, religious and geographical center of the city. Surrounding the other borders of the Zócalo are the National Palace (housing the offices of the president of Mexico), and other Federal government buildings.

A rainy evening in the Zócalo provides this majestic view of the historic Cathedral.

Mexico City, at night, becomes a glittering montage of activity. An exciting variety of entertainment and excellent cuisine is found in the many sophisticated night clubs located throughout the city. Many of these spots are ignited by the frequent presence of today's stars of the Mexican business and social worlds. Music comes in all guises from Spanish guitars and Flamenco dancers to the romantic "mariachis," and from esoteric jazz to the rock sound of the popular discotheques.

Pictured above is the colorful but intimate floor show at Gitanerías, one of the popular night spots, famous for its good food, drinks and lively Spanish shows. To the left is a pictorial study of feeling and intensity expressed in the artistic Flamenco dance performed at Gitanerías.

A soft-touch image complements the gentle lilting sounds of this rising new recording star of Mexico. Marián, a composer of most of her own music, entertains in many of the leading night spots of Mexico and Latin America.

Mexico offers a variety of continental cuisine. Representative of this palate-tempting art is the cookery available at LA CASSEROLE. Vol-au-vent Marinero, which contains red snapper, sea bass, oysters and shrimp in Nantua sauce and Baja California white wine (opposite page, top) contrasts with hardier staples of wine, vegetables, cheese dip and a freshly baked loaf of bread (opposite page, bottom).

Below, the table is set, ready for the most cultivated taste buds. Will you have the scallops in Spanish Macarelly drenched in white wine sauce au gratin or the duck livers cooked in red wine sauce and served in a pastry casserole?

EL CATORCE is now a ghost town but prior to the Revolution in 1910, Catorce's mines produced over 3 million dollars in high grade silver ore. It is so named because the region was the hideout of fourteen ("catorce" means fourteen) infamous bandits. While this is a familiar view of the Mexican countryside, reaching Catorce is a little out of the ordinary. Located on a mesa which is surrounded by ten thousand foot peaks, travelers must go the route by jeep . . . and the last two miles are through a tunnel of an old mine shaft.

Because the boom of industry is the heartbeat of
MONTERREY, it is known as the "Pittsburgh of
Mexico." While industrialization has made Monterrey
the second-ranking rail center in the country, an imprint
of Spanish colonial days still may be seen in the narrow
streets, flat-roofed houses, colorful patios, the cathedral
and some of the government buildings.

The Monterrey countryside is more . . . beautiful
Mexico. Below, the area near the famous Horsetail Falls
is shrouded in mist.

(Opposite page) The city of Monterrey lies in a great
valley at the foot of the Cerro de la Silla, (Saddle
Mountain), easily identified by its saddle-shaped crest.

Contributing to a 20th century Mexico on the move is the TRAILERS DE MONTERREY, S.A., truck, bus and parts factory in Monterrey. The firm turns out a wide variety of Ramírez diesel truck tractors and an assortment of trailers for them to pull, including freight boxes, tankers and panels.

They manufacture parts for trucks and automobile manufacturers, such as the Volkswagen plant in Puebla, and export to prime U.S. customers such as Ford Motor Company and American Motors Company.

Also produced here is a line of luxury highway buses marketed under the name Sultana. The mammoth highway cruisers feature four wheels in front and eight wheels in the back. The passenger level sits high off the ground by American standards. The ultimate in highway comfort, with galleys, stereo systems and air conditioning, they are designed to be manned by a driver and two attendants. The firm also makes more conventional city buses and smaller highway vehicles.

Left — a Ramírez truck and a Sultana bus roll off the line.

Sultana luxury buses receive finishing touches on the assembly line.

Bodies of Ramírez trucks undergo an inspection procedure before being mated with the proper power plant.

Cabs pictured on the assembly line move toward final phase of the manufacturing of the popular Mexican Ramírez truck.

Frames and other parts for various industrial vehicles to be assembled here and in other plants are manufactured in the Monterrey plant.

Lead crystalware from
the Monterrey plant,
CRISTALERIA, S.A., enjoys
international prestige
for quality and design.

Workman above manipulates a red hot glass mold that will soon become a work of art.

In the process a product is delicately ground by sensitive hands and modern machinery.

With the skill of a diamond cutter, this Cristalería craftsman cuts intricate facets into a beautiful decanter.

The Cristalería, S.A. Plant in Monterrey fired its first piece in 1936, and today manufactures some 48 million pieces a year. 1500 different standard pieces are made here, in addition to occasional custom or specially designed works.

The plant employs 3,000 craftsmen, designers and artisans. They mold 37,000 tons of glass each year. The product is marketed internationally under the Kristaluxus brand. Cristalería products annually compete with the best from hundreds of crystal factories all over the world, and consistently win top prizes at exhibitions.

The CONDUCTORES, S.A. plant is a high volume producer of wire, wire cables and other heavy industrial and electrical equipment, and is significant to Monterrey's reputation as Mexico's leading industrial city.

In the top picture at left, machines twist strands of wire into electrical cable while below, rolls of smaller wire, color coded to indicate sizes and specifications, wait for shipment.

A close-up study of thick copper strands used in heavy electrical cable.

Chilled mugs of Carta Blanca beer are a familiar and welcome sight to beer drinkers all over the world. The well-known brand is but one of many brews produced at Monterrey's CUAUHTEMOC, S.A. brewery, the largest in Mexico.

Below, the brewery welcomes all visitors, tourists as well as nationals, and offers an exquisite plaza in which to relax and sample the company's beer while enjoying the attractive atmosphere of the historic grounds and famous brewery building.

The luxury Vistadome train is seen on a journey into one of the North American continent's most exciting and spectacular frontiers of natural beauty. Mexico's "GRANDES BARRANCAS DE LA TARAHUMARA," a phenomenon of nature's scenic majesty, is a canyon complex four times larger than the Grand Canyon of the Colorado River. Labeled as one of the engineering feats of all time, the Chihuahua-Pacific Railroad is a 588-mile stretch of track spanning the rugged northern Sierra Madre mountains from east to west... the apotheosis of wilderness construction technology... tracks over 30 bridges and through 73 tunnels on a roadbed penetrating the pristine vistas of Mexico's grand canyons.

Following spread — A wide-angle camera lens view of Copper Canyon's regal terrain of plateaus and myriads of canyons, some two miles wide and one mile deep. The buildings seen in this picture are in DIVISADERO (which means "Lookout Point").

Divisadero was constructed on the rim of the Urique Canyon, which telescopes into the larger Cañon del Cobre . . . Copper Canyon. From the canyon floor some 6,000 feet below, Tarahumara Indians make the steep climb to the settlement to sell their handcraft wares to tourists. Colorfully attired Indian women and their babies are familiar sights in Divisadero. This is one of two lookout points located on the canyon tour.

A rocky lookout challenges the climber, then scales him
right back to puny insignificance in the grand landscape.
Opposite page — The Copper Canyon landscape is a
combination of shape and hue showing nature at her
passionate best.

A cathedral of canyon
monuments has been sculpted
over the centuries of time by
nature's hammer and chisel
of wind-blown abrasives,
sand and occasional
torrents of water. The
unexplored frontiers are a
bastion of Mexico's
tremendous reservoir of
natural resources waiting to
be explored and developed.

Looking straight down from Divisadero is an awe inspiring view of natural, primitive beauty and a window into ancient history as you see the home of the Tarahumara Indians, whose ancestors fled into the canyons from the Conquistadores in the late fifteenth and early sixteenth centuries. An estimated population of 55,000 Tarahumaras still live, as their predecessors did, in caves and crude stone houses, under cliff overhangs.

The canyon floor, some 6,000 feet below Divisadero, is a lush jungle where oranges, pineapples, mangoes, avocados, sugarcane and orchids grow wild. This virtual "Garden of Eden" is also the habitat of parrots and other brilliantly plumaged tropical birds, as well as wolves, panthers, coyotes, monkeys, jaguars, mountain lions, deer and fox. Man reigns supreme over this vast wilderness kingdom in the security of a life lived in the traditions and customs passed on by his ancestry.

The Tarahumara Indian is recognized principally for his handicrafts and his running ability. Tarahumara, or Raramuri, translated in English, is footrunner. With their great endurance, the men can outrun the deer. They hunt in the canyon and have been known to race for 72 hours at top speed during special tribal celebrations.

The artistic study pictured at the right is a canyon moss, found specifically in this region, which grows on the canyon walls, rocks and trees.

GUAYMAS, located on the Sea of Cortés in the state of Sonora, is one of Mexico's well known seaports. An indulgent coast of beaches and tepid blue waters add to its appeal as a popular resort center. Guaymas is actually two communities, the city with its cathedral, fishing docks, freighters and tankers in the harbor, divided by a mountainous peninsula from the resort area along Bacochibampo Bay.

Small boats bob gently in the bay at CABO
SAN LUCAS, on the very tip of Baja. Visible
on the other side of the bay are luxurious
tourist hotels, built into the cliffsides.

Hotel builders, seeking to impress the visitor
with the atmosphere of the bay, have sunk
the structures into the cliff faces.

Sandy beaches complement the scenic
wonder of rocky cliffs and rolling surf.

The Baja Highway is a combination of
excellent two lane roads and expressways
that extend from the U.S. border all the way
to the tip of the Baja Peninsula (left). This
stretch is between La Paz and Cabo San
Lucas. Along the way are pleasant rest stops
and hotels, such as this one in BUENA
VISTA, which features deluxe
accommodations, a pool and an inviting
view of the Pacific.

LA PAZ, located on the coast of the Baja Peninsula, is a world famous sport fishing center.

Below — A charter party visits one of several small islands dotting the sea around La Paz after a morning of exciting fishing. Beaches in this area are sprinkled with a myriad of gaily colored shells, which are a treat for the collector.

An artistic view of La Paz harbor.

The BAJA HIGHWAY (Mex. Route 1), pictured, is a section between the U.S. border and Ensenada.

Pictured at right . . . Rosarito Beach, enroute to Ensenada, has long been a favorite vacation beach for Mexicans and visiting Californians. Pacesetting new housing is changing the residential and business profile into a model of economic progress, while preserving the traditional tourist appeal.

Top — The Tijuana Jai Alai Fronton Palace operates nightly year 'round except Thursdays. Over a half million people visit it and more than $100,000 is distributed in payoffs to lucky winners every week. This pari-mutuel betting concession is one of the few authorized by the Mexican Federal Government.

Jai Alai is justifiably called the world's fastest game . . . the ball attains speeds up to 165 mph. Left — The court is 40 feet wide, 40 feet high and 180 feet long. Players bounce the ball off the walls, using carom shots to increase the velocity to blinding speed.

Pictured on the steps at the entrance of the ornately decorated Fronton Palace are three of Jai Alai's most popular "pelotari" (the athletes who play). The sport, a very dangerous and thrilling one, originated four centuries ago in the Basque provinces of Spain. Modern day Jai Alai is played internationally.

The art and ritual of bullfighting dates back to 2,000 years before Christ. It features three main acts: Picadors, on horses, lance the bull to weaken its neck muscles; the Banderilleros, on foot, place a pair of darts in the bull; the Matador enters alone on foot, carrying a sword and a muleta, a small red cloth draped over a stick. Thus begins the ballet of death . . . a contest between a man and his courage, rather than just between a man and a bull. This event epitomizes the Mexican philosophy of flirting and laughing at death and danger.

In the top picture the Matador, a poised silhouette of resolute courage and agile grace, challenges one of the famed fighting bulls of Mexico to make a pass.

Bottom, the crowd roars its approval of the Matador's courage.

Left —— In this aerial view of Tijuana, a point of particular note is the bullfighting ring, which appears as a white bowl on an apron of asphalt. Bottom left —— Looking down into the valley, the oblong shaped circle in the distance is the famous Caliente Race Track, in Tijuana. Adding a fantasy mood to these pictures, a low vaporous lacey white cloud moves in from the ocean and settles over sections of the city like an ethereal bridal veil.
Below — The border crossing at San Diego and Tijuana logs thousands of visitors each month.

Next page —
A Mexican sunset (this one at La Paz) gives an almost spiritual meaning to "Mañana."

A Mexican sunset speaks to many in the reverent terms of an inspirational experience. It is like a prayer of benediction at the end of the day. Warm with the anticipation of faith, hope and confidence that "mañana's" sunrise will bring the promise of a brighter, better day for Mexico and the world.

Muchas Gracias
Vaya Con Dios

THE PHOTOGRAPHER

The man chosen by Licenciado Miguel Aleman to capture on film, the fire, excitement and beauty of Mexico Today, is JURGIS MOTIEKAITIS.

Jurgis is a designer, art major and Lithuania's "crowned prince" of natural light photography. He was born into the royal lineage of the Fine Arts . . . His father, Walter Motiekaitis is listed in the Lithuanian encyclopedia as their most famous Concert Master and Solo Violinist, standing shoulder to shoulder with the musical giants of his generation, such as Fritz Kreisler. His brother is currently the Principal Cellist of the Internationally renowned Sydney, Australia Symphony Orchestra.

Motiekaitis, who is rapidly becoming known as one of the world's foremost photographers, releases his creative genius in an "orchestration" of photographic moods and designs of unduplicated beauty.

Jurgis Motiekaitis says . . . "I chose the Honeywell Pentax 6 x 7 cameras and lenses for this assignment because, in my opinion, it is the finest equipment on the market."

PHOTOGRAPHER'S COMMENTARY

This commentary is dedicated to everyone who is interested in photography. The subsequent material includes information pertinent to the pictures in this publication. If the written text creates the impression that you are looking at the subjects photographed in Mexico through the lens with me, our objective will have, in part, been achieved. It is also my intention to share with you some of my convictions on the prudent selection and purchase of photography equipment, the philosophy of composition and the art of directing.

I have used, in the course of my professional career, almost all of the well-known cameras, and discovered that the approximate average life of a camera body is two years. As a commercial photographer, you must have dependable equipment. My assignments are often in some of the most primitive and remote areas of the globe, and under conditions that allow only one opportunity to capture the subject on film. The costs are horrendous and there is no margin allowed for equipment failure.

Hopefully the proceeding narration has cogently established some reasons for purchasing the best photography equipment money can buy. The conditions imposed on the photography phase in the production of "PICTORIAL IMAGES OF MEXICO TODAY" demanded that a normal year's work be compressed into 90 days. After carefully looking at the latest equipment on the market, in the context of quality and dependability, Honeywell Pentax's 6 x 7 was selected as the only camera for this formidable task. The 35mm camera had previously been my preference. However, I found the amazing format and mobility of the Honeywell Pentax made the transition from the 35mm easy. After some familiarity tests, using the 6 x 7, I felt equally confident and comfortable with either camera. Honeywell Pentax lenses are as good or, in my opinion, superior to any camera lenses manufactured. When you look through a 6 x 7 lens the difference might be compared to opening the door to see the view opposed to squinting through the key hole.

Speaking of mobility, the average photographer can, with dependability, hand hold a 6 x 7 for up to a 15th of a second. I can personally hand hold the camera at an 8th of a second without even giving a thought to the use of a tripod and guarantee 100% efficiency. We used Kodak's Ektachrome 120 ASA 64 film. When it comes to viewing and editing the 2¼ x 2¾ size negatives, they are a breeze compared to monitoring 35mm slides. Further, enlarging pictures to be used in a double page spread can become marginal with 35mm film.

May we focus our attention for a moment on the use of light meters. For natural light photography, it has always been my philosophy that the seasoned and experience-trained eye of the photographer is the only answer for consistent optimum results in natural light photography. The theory is now being taught currently in the renowned schools of photography. Most assuredly the light meter is an invaluable piece of equipment and is the answer when you are left to the mercy of artificial light. However, may we emphasize, bracket every shot two or three stops. Bracketing is the best insurance in the world and is always practiced by seasoned professionals. I personally prefer to work with negatives a stop or two darker than the natural "right on" density. Some clients request that the subject be shot lighter than the natural density. Remember, color values can be extracted in the processing of the film, but can never be added. A degree of darkness in pictures can give them a Rembrandt painting quality, while at the other end of the spectrum, a picture shot 3 stops lighter can result in a beautiful soft touch effect. Although you can normally get good average pictures there is no versatility in shooting strictly with a light meter, because the readings preserve a constant light value under normal natural light circumstances. I encourage you to accept the challenge of learning the "no light meter" natural light technique if your goal is to become known as a true artist. You are a professional the day that you become the master of your equipment, and the prevailing conditions you are confronted with on assignments. The professional is never left to the mercy of whether it is an ideal day for photography or to the mechanical sterility of his equipment. Any circumstance presents the opportunity of taking a super shot when experience adds the ingredients of composition and the proper exposure.

The importance of purchasing photography equipment that is of the finest and most durable quality was emphasized earlier in this commentary. However, as we prepare to address ourselves to the vital subject of composition it is only proper to state, equipment is not an end unto itself in the creation of prize winning or artistically acceptable pictures. Almost anyone can load film into an expensive camera, follow the instructions for making the mechanical adjustments, point it and flick the shutter. However, the camera, like the surgeon's scalpel, is merely an instrument. The results are governed by the training, experience and natural artistic gifts of the photographer. The preceding paragraph is preparatory to the importance of our next topic, composition.

Although people may be endowed genetically with natural artistic aptitudes that contribute to good composition, extraordinary composition is the product of experience and academic discipline. Composition may be defined as one line or many lines and shapes that form a single unit. Excellent composition can transform a boring subject and dull color into a masterpiece of exciting beauty. The element of composition is, in my opinion, the most important factor in creating a superior painting or photograph. If you have the facility for recognizing the ingredients of good composition, as you look through the camera lens, your pictures will delight an art director because, the message is artistically composed in the picture. Frequently, the question is asked, "Is it possible for everyone to take pictures?" The answer is obviously yes. However, if the implication of the question is, can just anyone pick up a camera and without a background of experience or training take professional pictures, the answer is, emphatically NO!! If the pictures you have taken, as an amateur, are well composed you have a natural gift that will aid you in becoming a professional photographer. When I look through the lens at the subject to be photographed, whether it is industry, models or scenery, I only see shapes and lines crossing each other. If all these lines and shapes form a beautiful composition, then the picture is a winner, regardless of the subject. The question I am often asked is, "What camera did you use to shoot this super shot?" The super shot is a product of total dedication and devotion to the disciplines of the art of photography.

As an example, in reviewing the situations we faced in Mexico, The Yucatán Peninsula and the city of Mérida, were a challenge because we were there during the dry season. The pyramids and ruins at Chichén Itzá were grey and dull looking in color. The sky was light blue and the vegetation around the ruins were dry and grey with small patches of green sparsely scattered. Since we could not wait for better conditions in order to get a good picture of the pyramids, I shot them in a soft-touch greeting card style. The same dry conditions and limited time factors made the coverage of Tulúm (pg. 31b) a problem in composition and technique. We arrived late in the afternoon and I only had 15 minutes of daylight to capture the drama and beauty of this historic subject. To accomplish this I over-exposed the shot to give it an amber soft touch effect. Another set of circumstances confronted me at the ruins near Poza Rica, called El Tajín (pg. 50 & 51). The morning fog was lifting with a gorgeous sunrise peaking through. To catch the mystical mood of ancient history in this situation, I again over-exposed all my shots.

In Cancún, everything is white except for the blue sky and turquoise water. Since my intention was to show the color of the water and not the white sand, I ended up shooting at 60 - 16, and at 125 - 16 which produced colorful pictures emphasizing the blue of water and sky contrasting, the white sandy beaches.

The church at Campeche was also photographed on a drab overcast day making a dead composition of beige buildings against the hazy sky. To bring life and excitement into the picture I found an interesting angle, bringing the varied hues of the surrounding foliage into the composition. The leaves in the foreground and the trees in the park had many shades of green and properly used brought color into the picture. Waiting for a beautiful day or the perfect situation is a luxury a commercial photographer or even a beginner 5000 miles from home cannot afford. It is your artistic composition that will make your picture look good, regardless.

Experience in industrial photography and the use of proper safety procedures and equipment in an oil industry picture can make or break your shot. As an example, you may have a great picture of a beautiful refinery with men working in the foreground, but if one man in the crowd has no hard hat or someone has a cigarette in his mouth, you might as well forget it. This picture will end up in the trash can.

Azufrera Panamericana (APSA) was excited about my art direction of their workers and knowledge of the safety rules. Sometimes, looking out for one's own personal safety can be a ticklish situation. For instance, at A.P.S.A. in Jaltipan, Veracruz, I was kneeling and finally lying down in patches of grass on a soft hill, shooting steam rising from the ground along with men working on a "Christmas tree," (drilling rig). When I finally finished and walked away, I discovered I was carrying a disease called "5,000 ants all over my body." They were crawling in my shorts, inside my shirt and in my boots, I was covered with live ants. Oh, well . . . it was an exciting day . . . not for me, but for the Mexican workers who were hysterically laughing at me. Often on industrial assignments, the action may not be on the subject you must photograph. This is the reason the ability to set up your shot is vital in being a professional photographer. For example, when we were photographing at APSA, the workmen had been called off the steam drilling rig which had been scheduled to be photographed for our coverage of the company. They were working at another site on something else. The picture on pages 44 & 45 is the result of delicate diplomacy and professional direction. I positioned the men on the drilling rig in working postures pushing and pulling levers and using tools with strenuous efforts that caused their muscles to bulge and facial expressions to grimace under the strain. If it is possible, I film natural action, however, knowledge of art direction and the devices of superior composition are critical to getting in, taking your picture and moving on to the next subject. There is still no better method than a bucket of water poured on a workman to produce the appearance of a sweat drenched laborer. A word of caution, however, with his permission . . . of course. At the Atenquíque wood pulp factory, the procedure was reversed and the photographer took a bath (page 78). I laid down on the ground and asked the worker to take a shovel and bury me with wood pulp chips. This was a stop action shot at a setting of 250 - 8. The pictures taken of the Copper Canyon were shot from a platform on the front of the diesel engine of a fast moving train, as I clung for 8 hours to my camera with one hand and precariously balanced myself with the other. The train was traveling from Chihuahua to its first scheduled stop at Divisadero. To compensate for the speed of the train, I shot at 500 - 5.6 and 250 - 8.

Upon arrival at Divisadero, I spent the balance of the day filming the panoramic scenery with the huge fluffy clouds as accents and finally ended a long day with pictures of the late evening sun. When people photograph mountains, they almost always look for a spectacular panoramic view. This makes sense, but they often overlook the more subtle yet equally as interesting subjects. As I was walking through this "Grand Canyon" of Mexico looking for some good and different panoramic pictures, I became intrigued by the gorgeous light green moss growing on the bark of the trees, rocks and canyon walls. A close up study (pg. 293) of this unusual moss provided a different artistic perspective to this magnificent canyon.

The potentials for photography in Mexico are good all year around and present a challenging artistic frontier for cameramen to explore. It is not true that only November through February are the best months for photography. April through September is Mexico's rainy season and provides the opportunity of filming your subjects using the backdrop of stunning transitions of mood in sky and cloud formations. The variations run the gamut from blue skies with fluffy white clouds to grey tempestuous black storm clouds and finally the wonder of golden clouds in early evening skies. In the vicinity of Mexico City, you will find a variety of topography from "Swiss Alps" mountain scenery to desert land, and luxuriant tropical vegetation.

The Switzerland atmosphere may be found approximately three hours drive from Mexico City on the road to Avándaro, or in a one hour drive west of Tepoztlán. Tropical flora is located in Fortín De Las Flores (The Garden Town) a short drive from Mexico City. On the highway to Acapulco and Pachuca is where you may find desert scenery.

We have included the aperture setting, for your interest, of each picture used in "Pictorial Images of Mexico Today." The pursuit of new vistas of expertise and artistry in my profession, is the singular goal and interest of my life. This is the formula common to becoming a super star in any profession . . . dedication, indefatigable work and determination. Speaking as one photographer to another, I close now with the wish that all of the "negatives" in your life develop into beautiful "positives" of real life portraits.

INDEX OF PICTURES AND CAMERA SETTINGS

All shots taken with Takumar 55mm wide angle lens unless otherwise specified

Page	Shutter Speed	F-Stop	Subject
2-3	125	22	Silver clouds and sun star
7	30	3.5	Miguel Aleman
10	60	16-22	El Presidente hotel beach and umbrellas
11A	60	16-22	Cozumel beach and tree
11B	60	16	Pool at El Presidente Hotel
13A	60	16	Cozumel beach and rocky cove
13B	60	11	Cozumel sunset and boats
14	125	11	Pilot and plane
15A	60	16	Cozumel airport
15B	500	5.6	Aerial view of Cozumel
16A	125	16	Cancun — huts and beach
16B	60	16	Cancun — car, boat and sandy cove
17	125	16	Cancun beach and Mayan statue
18-19	500	5.6	Aerial view of Cancun
20A	500	5.6	Aerial view of Isla Mujeres
20B	60	16	Lagoon with boat and scuba divers
21	60	16	Hotel viewed through fish net
22	60	16	Monument in Merida
23A	60	16	Colorful Merida street scene
23B	60	11	Modern house in Merida
23C	60	16	Colonial house viewed through iron
24-25	2,1,5,10	3.5	Cordomex factory (35% yellow filter)
26	60	16	Henequen plant in monument at Cordomex
27A	60	16	Cordomex factory grounds
27B	250	5.6	Jaguar
27C	60	16	Guest house pool at Cordomex
28-29	60	16	Chichen Itza ruins
30A	60	16	Arches at Uxmal ruins
30B	60	16	Pyramid at Uxmal
31A	60	16	Pyramid at Chichen Itza
31B	60	5.6	Tulum ruins
32	60	16	Church and modern ramp at Campeche
34	60	16	Drilling rig framed by palm leaves
35	125	5.6	Villahermosa girl in red dress
36A	4,2,1,5,10	3.5	Mal Paso generator room
36B	4,2,1,5,10	3.5	Mal Paso control room
36C	30	3.5	Mal Paso power station
36D	4,2,1,5,10	3.5	Mal Paso lower generator room
37	60	3.5	View of Mal Paso Dam
38A	8	3.5	Pemex laboratory
38B	60	16	View of refinery in Minititlan
39	60	16	Design shot of refinery
40	60	16	Pemex station
41	60	16	Pemex workers at refinery
42-43	15,8,4	3.5	Night shot at Veracruz
44-45	500	5.6	Men on drilling rig at A.P.S.A.
46A	60	16	A.P.S.A. over view
46B	60	16	Tanks reflected in water
47A	60	16	Sulfur stock piled near rails
47B	125	11	Portrait of sulphur worker
46-47	250	8	Men working at sulphur steam well
49	60	16	Picture of worker through wheel
50	60	5.6	El Tajin ruins (Kodachrome II)
51	60	11	Pyramid at El Tajin (Kodachrome II)
52	15,8,4,2	3.5	City of Poza Rica at night
53A	60	11	Gas torches at Poza Rica
53B	60	3.5	Reflection of light from gas flame
54	60	16	Church in Oaxaca
55	60	3.5	Black pottery in Oaxaca
56	30	3.5	Girl in Oaxacan folk dress (135mm lens)
57A	60	3.5	Hotel in Oaxaca
57B	60	16	Hotel pool in Oaxaca
58A	60	16	Monte Alban ruins
58B	60	16	Mitla ruins and colonial church in background
59A	60	16	Small town church
59B	15	3.5	Tule tree
60	500	5.6	Acapulco diver
61	60	16	Cross and hands
62-63A	4,2,1,5,10	3.5	Acapulco bay at night
62-63B	60	16	Acapulco bay in daytime
64	125	11	Man cutting coconut

Page	Shutter Speed	F-Stop	Subject
69A	60	16	Man cutting La Concha shell
69B	60	16	View of La Concha beach club
69C	250	8	Picture of para-sailor
70	30	3.5	Modern sculpture in convention center
70-71	60	16	Convention center amphitheater
71	60	16	Outside view of convention center
72-73	60	16	Zihuatanejo beach
74	60	16	Las Truchas steel mill
76	60	16	Ship in Las Truchas harbor
77A	60	16	Steel construction
77B	15	3.5	Young men working on machines
78	250	8	Man shoveling wood chips
79	60	16	Over view of Atenquique factory
80A	60	16	Wood pulp stock piled
80B	250	8	Truck being unloaded
81A	60	11	Housing at Atenquique
81B	125	11	Children coming home from school at Atenquique
82-83	60	16-22	Manzanillo harbor
84-85	60	5.6	Las Hadas Hotel in Manzanillo
86	60	11	Guadalajara cathedral
87A	60	16	Girl stepping out of carriage
87B	60	16	Minerva statue
87C	60	11	Arches in Guadalajara
87D	60	16	Art center building
88A	15	3.5	Inside view of Hospicio Cabañas orphanage
88B	30	3.5	View of Orozco mural in orphanage
89	60	16	Children at entrance of orphanage
90	60	8	Girl in charro costume
91	60	3.5	Portrait of Guadalajara girl (135mm lens)
92A	125	8	Beer product shot
92B	60	16	Outside view of Guadalajara brewery
93A	30	3.5	Bottling assembly line
93B	60	8	View of brewery pipes and tanks
94ABC	8,4,2,1	3.5	Kodak processing and packaging
94D	Flash	—	Man working at Kodak
95A	125	3.5	Glass artisan viewed through arches (135mm lens)
95B	15	3.5	Glass bull (135mm lens)
95C	15	3.5	View of glass artisan
96A	60	3.5	Lookout point of canyon
96B	60	16	Waterfall
97A	125	5.6	Carved mangos on sticks
97B	60	16-22	Boats on Lake Chapala
98	60	4	Portrait of old man in Puerto Vallarta (Kodachrome II)
100	60	11	Sunset in Puerto Vallarta (Kodachrome II)
101	60	11	Puerto Vallarta lagoon (Kodachrome II)
102A	60	8	Banana man
102B	60	16	Banana plantation scene
103A	125	11	Tobacco and cigarette product shot
103B	60	16	Traditional Huichol Indian costume
104A	60	11	Mazatlan cathedral (Kodachrome II)
104B	60	11	Boats on Mazatlan beach (Kodachrome II)
105A	60	16	Seafood platter
105B	125	11	Man preparing game fish to be mounted
106A	125	3.5	Product shot of canned sardines (135mm lens)
106B	60	3.5	Product shot of frozen shrimp
107	60	11	Labeled cans of sardines on boats
108-109	60	11	Durango mountain road (polarizing filter and Kodachrome II)
110	60	3.5	Girl's portrait
111	60	3.5	Model in white leather suit
112	30	3.5	Product shot of shoes
113A	15	3.5	Girl working with white shoes
113B	8	3.5	Cobbler working on boots
113C	4	3.5	Cobbler sewing shoes
114A	4,2,1,5,10	3.5	Man inspecting leather (pink filter 35%)
114B	4,2,1,5,10	3.5	Cutting room (pink filter 35%)
115ABC	2,1,5,10	3.5	Shoe production line
116	60	16	Road scene to Guanajuato
117A	60	16	Countryside view of hut and mountains
117B	60	16	Boy tending cattle on a hillside
118-119	60	22-16	Scenic view of church and mountains overlooking Guanajuato
120	125	8	Papiermache statue of Don Quixote
121	60	11	Panoramic view of Guanajuato
122	60	16	View looking down into subterranean road
123	30,15,8,4	3.5	Night shot of subterranean road
124A	60	16	Design shot of Juarez Theater
124B	15,4,8,2	3.5	Interior view of Juarez Theater

Page	Shutter Speed	F-Stop	Subject
125	60	16	Over view of two famous hotels in Guanajuato
126A	60	5.6	Soft touch boy-girl shot (135mm lens using cellophane paper around lens)
126B	60	8	Picturesque plaza in Guanajuato
127	125	11	Boy and girl walking down narrow street
128	60	16	Flower cart
129A	125	11	Silver jewelry (135mm lens)
129B	125	3.5	Portrait of lady in red shawl
130-131A	2,1,5,10	3.5	Salamanca refinery at night
130-131B	15	3.5	Control room at refinery
132	60	16	Church viewed through wrought iron fence
133	4,2,1,5,10	3.5	Interior of church
134	60	16	Tomato field with cactus in foreground
135	60	5.6	Farmer with tractor
136A	125	11	Workers in field (135mm lens)
136B	60	16	Boxes of green tomatoes
137	125	11	Workers in tomato field
138	60	16	Conasupo stone bins
139A	125	3.5	Farmer looking at citrus trees
139B	125	11	Hands cutting fruit
139C	125	11	Farmer and son looking at crops
140	60	16	Town plaza viewed through arches
142-143	60	22-16	View of Lake Jurica
144A	60	5.6	Boy and girl balancing on aqueduct
144B	60	16	Landscaped view of aqueduct
145A	60	16	Pool and umbrella area of Hotel Jurica
145B	4,2	3.5	Interior view of hotel dining room
145C	125	3.5	Picture of wrangler and horse
145D	250	8	Man serving tennis
146	60	16	Stone archway at Tequisquiapan
147	60	16	Luxurious home in Tequisquiapan
148A	15	3.5	Interior of home
148B	8	3.5	Interior of home
149	60	11	Tequisquiapan home and pool
150	60	16	Red flower in foreground of golf fairway
151	60	16	Avandaro lake and mountain area
152	60	16	Pool area and golf fairway at Avandaro
153A	250	8	Golfer teeing off
153B	60	8	Avandaro club house and game room
154-155	60	16	Hillside view of Taxco
156	60	5.6	Silver tray of Taxco
157A	8	3.5	Furniture
157B	125	5.6	Silver rosary
157C	60	3.5	Indian rug
158A	8	3.5	Interior view of Palafox library
158B	60	5.6	Tile work in courtyard
159	60	16	Cathedral of Puebla
159	60	11	Church decorated with the tile of Puebla
160	60	16	Stacks of colorful pottery
161A	4	3.5	Potters working at wheel
161B	125	11	Man painting large vase
162	60	16	Volkswagen plant of Mexico
163A	60	16	Volkswagen bumpers
163B	60	16	Volkswagen headlight and plant
163C	60	16	VW Plant with flowers in foreground
164-165	15,8,4,2	3.5	VW foundry
166A	15	3.5	VW production line
166B	8	3.5	Stack of front fenders
167A	15	3.5	Welder on assembly line
167B	4	3.5	Stock of painted fenders and chassis
168-169	60	16	Church on top of hill
170-171A	60	16	Old and new bridges
170-171B	60	16	Cornfield and volcanic peak in the distance
172-173	60	16	Mexico City panorama
174-175	60	16	Picture of Angel and city in background
176	60	16	44 story Latin American Tower
177	60	16	Hotel Mexico
178	60	16	Siqueiros Cultural Polyforum
179	60	16	Palace of Fine Arts
180	60	16	View of Basilica of Guadalupe
181	125	11	Chapel of the Little Well (135mm lens)
182	60	16	Modern building with flag covering it
183A	60	16	Colonial style building viewed through wrought iron
183B	60	16	Plaza of Three Cultures
184	60	8	Pemex monument
185A	60	16	Fountain and sculpture
185B	60	11	Fountain and pool

Page	Shutter Speed	F-Stop	Subject
186A	60	16	Statue on balcony overlooking city
186B	60	16	Chapultepec Castle
187A	125	11	Children running through wooded park
187B	125	8	Cotton candy man and balloons
187C	250	8	Kids playing soccer in park
188A	4,2,1	3.5	View of sewer tunnel under construction
188B	60	16	Group of engineers talking
188C	60	5.6	Welder working in tunnel
189C	8,4,2	3.5	Large view of tunnel and rails
189B	60	16	Tunnel workers outside
190A	60	16	Apartments in Mexico
190B	60	16	Modern home
190C	60	16	Community street and homes in Mexico
191ABC	60	16	Modern Spanish style homes in new Mexican housing community
192A	125	11	Bus in Mexico City
192B	4	3.5	Subway
193	125	11	Taxi in traffic
194	15	3.5	Chandelier in department store
195A	8	3.5	Shopping mall store window
195B	4	3.5	View of stores in mall
196A	30	3.5	Fish and wine display in window
196B	60	8	Dresses on a mannequin in window
196C	15	3.5	Display of silver jewelry
197A	15	3.5	Street reflections in store window
197B	125	8	Sidewalk cafe on street
197C	60	16	Corner of exclusive shopping area
198	30	3.5	Model in white dress (135mm lens)
199	60	8	Model in red dress (Kodachrome II)
200	125	5.6	Picture of white hibiscus flower
201A	60	8	Ladies shopping at flower market
201B	60	5.6	Man arranging flowers
201C	60	8	Close up of flower basket
202-203	125	3.5	Mariachis (Kodachrome II)
204A	125	3.5	Woman cooking and serving food
204B	125	3.5	Pineapple decorated with shrimp and cherries
204C	125	5.6	Fountain decorated with fruit
205A	60	11	Small sculptures for sale at bazaar
205B	60	5.6	Lamps viewed through red color
205C	60	11	Copper kettles and wicker baskets
206A	60	11	Courtyard of San Angel Inn
206B	4	3.5	Interior of San Angel Inn restaurant
207A	125	8	Red drink
207B	125	11	Lobster dish
208	60	5.6	Umbrella at Museum of Anthropology
209	15	3.5	Portrait of architect
210-211	60	16	Outside view of entrance to the Museum
212	15,8,4,2	3.5	Large green head
214	15,8,4,2	3.5	Main hall of museum
215ABCD	15,8,4,2	3.5	Mural and display of Tomb of Palenque
216	60	16	Outside view of school
217A	60	11	View of school classrooms outside
217B	60	16	View of playing field and school
218-219	60	16	University library building
221	60	16	University administration building
222	60	16	University medical building
223A	15	3.5	Interior of classroom at university
223B	4	3.5	University medical laboratory
223C	4	3.5	University engineering laboratory
224A	60	11	Nuclear plant administration building
224B	60	11	Over view of nuclear plant
225A	4,2,1,5	3.5	Technician working nuclear materials
225B	30	3.5	Outside view of nuclear reactor
225C	15,8,4,2	3.5	Looking down into the nuclear reactor
226C	60	16	Medical center entrance
226B	60	16	Medical center doctors
227ABC	8,4,2,1,5	3.5	Hospital laboratory and equipment (35% pink filter)
228AB	15	3.5	Dentist working on patient in office
231	125	5.6	Hearing doctor with children
232A	250	3.5	Little boy with mother and teacher
232B	8	3.5	Doctor speaking with lab technicians
233ABC	250	3.5	Series of pictures of little boy
234	60	3.5	Industrial exposition over view
235	60	5.6	Individual exhibitor's display
236A	8	3.5	Industrialist talking to foreman
236B	15	3.5	Over view of furniture plant
237A	15,8,4,2	3.5	Industrialist looking at console
237B	15,8,4,2	3.5	Laminating machines for Briomica
237C	15,8,4,2	3.5	BrioTubo tubing factory
238-239	15,8,4,2	3.5	Folklorico dancers

Page	Shutter Speed	F-Stop	Subject
240ABC	125	3.5	Folklorico dancers (Ektachrome ASA 125)
241	15	3.5	Man in sombrero (Ektachrome ASA 125)
242	60	5.6	Dancer in white dress
243A	60	3.5	Portrait of dancer's face
243B	250	8	Girl dancing in red folklorico dress
244	250	8	Charro on horse performing
245	125	11	Study of sombrero rope and gloves (135mm lens)
246A	125	3.5	Young charro
246B	125	5.6	Old charro
247	55	5.6	Charros roping horse (135mm lens)
248A	250	8	Tennis players on court
248B	60	3.5	Girl and tennis racket
249A	60	8	Crowds at race track
249B	500	3.5	Jockey passing grandstands
249C	500	3.5	Horses crossing finish line
250	125	3.5	Aztec soccer stadium
251ABC	250	5.6	Young men playing soccer
252A	125	3.5	Young people's chamber music concert
252BCDE	Used floods and meter reading		Close up study of young musicians
253	250	3.5	Close up of orchestra conductor
254	250	8	Classical quartet
255	30	3.5	Portrait of solo cellist
256	60	5.6	Group shot of water color artists
257ABC	60	5.6	Pictures of various artists
258	15,8,4,2	3.5	Night street scene
259	15,8,4,2	3.5	Night street scene
260-261	30,15,4	3.5	Night shot of cathedral
262A	15	3.5	Night club floor show
262B	30	3.5	Flamenco dancer
263	60	5.6	Soft touch shot of girl with guitar (Used cellophane wrapped around lens)
264AB			
265	Used floods, meter reading and bracketing		Shots of food
266-267	60	16	Church (Orange filter)
269	60	16	View of saddle back mountain
268	15	3.5	Foggy mist and trees (Kodachrome II)
270A	60	5.6	Truck
270B	15	3.5	Bus on assembly line
272A	8	3.5	Buses on assembly line
272B	8	3.5	Truck assembly line
273A	4	3.5	Cabs of trucks on assembly line
273B	125	11	Tow motor lifting trailer frames
274-275	4,2,1,5,10	3.5	Production shot of crystal
276ABC	4,2,1,5,10	3.5	Man working with hot glass and crystal being cut
277ABC	4,2,1,5,10	3.5	Series of finished glass products
278A	15	3.5	Electrical cable production line
278B	15	3.5	Spools of colorful wire
279	8	3.5	Close up study of copper cable
280	60	5.6	Close up study of beer
281	60	5.6	Plaza of brewery
282	500	5.6	Train going through canyon scenery
282	500	5.6	Rails and tunnel
284-285	60	11	Panoramic view of Divisadero
286	60	16	Indian woman with baby on back
287	60	22-16	View of Divisadero area
288	60	16	Panorama of mountain canyon
289	60	16	Boy standing on large boulder
290-291	60	16	Mountain panorama
293	15	3.5	Green moss on tree
294	60	11	Palm lined beach scene (Kodachrome II)
295A	60	11	Hillside view of Guaymas city
295B	250	8	Boys and man tossing fish into pans
296-297	60	16	Boats in harbor of Cabo San Lucas
297ABC	60	5.6	Pictures of hotels and beach at Cabo San Lucas
298	60	16-22	Desert road scene in Baja California
299	60	8	Pool side view of ocean
300A	125	11	Man pulling in fish
300B	60	16-22	Boat, fish and fishing boat on beach
301	60	16	Boat and harbor seen through rope
302	60	16	Baja road and bridge
303A	60	16	Rosarita beach homes and lantern
303B	60	16-22	Sea side beach scene
304A	60	16	Front of Jai Alai palace
304B	8	3.5	Playing court of Jai Alai
304C	125	11	Shot of Jai Alai players
305ABC	250	5.6	Bullfighter and crowds (Kodachrome II)
306A	500	5.6	Aerial view of Tijuana bullfight ring
306B	60	11	Hillside view of Caliente race track and foggy Tijuana valley (135mm lens)
307	500	5.6	Aerial of Tijuana and San Diego border crossing
308-309	60	16-22	Sunset shot of La Paz harbor

ACKNOWLEDGEMENTS

The success of a project like Pictorial Images of Mexico Today would not be possible without the faith, patience, cooperation and hard work of countless people both in Mexico and the United States. There are neither sufficient words nor space to adequately express proper gratitude to all of those who contributed their part to the completion of this publication.

For vital assistance and collaboration in Mexico we wish to express deep appreciation to *Licenciado Miguel Alemán,* Presidente del Consejo Nacional de Turismo and members of his excellent staff. In particular, Coordinator General, *Sr. Miguel Guajardo,* Sub-Coordinator General, *Sr. Guillermo Moreno* and Director of Foreign Affairs, *Sr. Enrique Monroy.* A special word of thanks to *Srta. Elena E. Hannan* for special editorial and technical assistance and *Sr. Jorge Sendel,* our liaison assigned to this project by Consejo Nacional de Turismo. Sr. Sendel is the Mexican promotion and public relations director for Pictorial Images of Mexico Today.

Other special assistance was rendered by *Sna. Gheane Briones de Maksimow;* without her dedication and hard work this publication would not have been completed. In addition we are grateful to *Mr. Walter Maksimow* for his contributions and to our excellent pilot and friend, *Captain Gustavo Lomelí.*

In the United States many rendered invaluable help in their particular field of expertise: Business Consultant — *Mr. Rick Bowler;* Art — *Mrs. Jean Thornburg* and *Mr. Richard A. Maynard;* Editorial — *Tom* and *Phyllis Durkin.* We owe a deep debt of gratitude to *Mr. Tony Velez* who was responsible for our initial contact in Mexico.

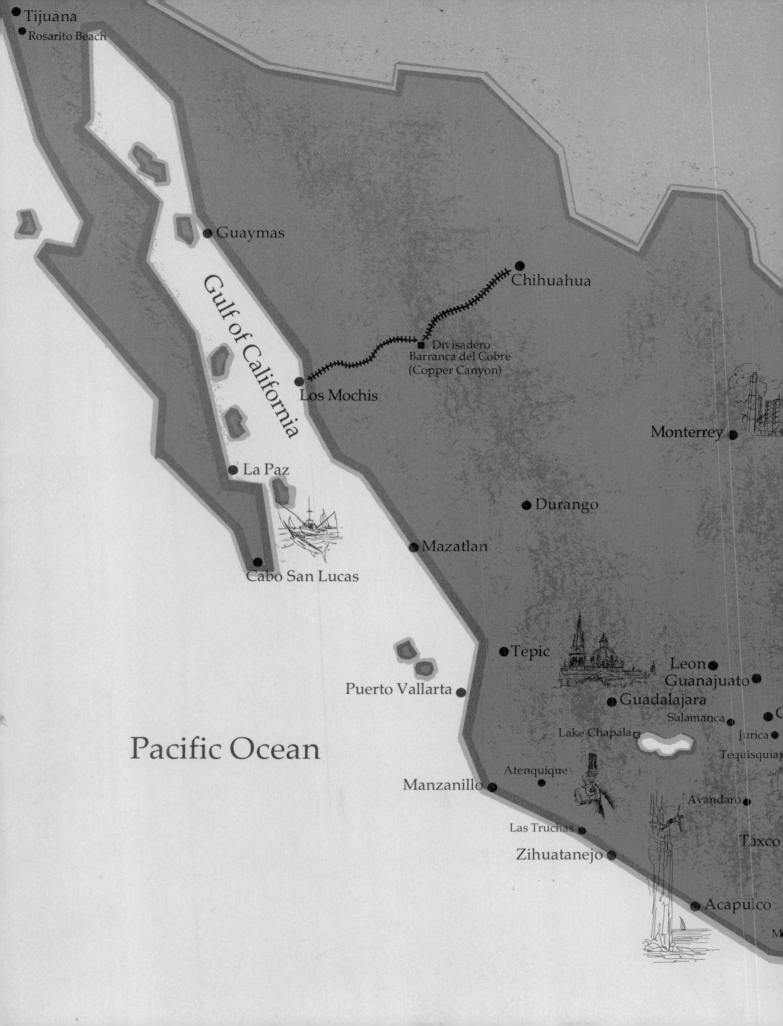

Tijuana
Rosarito Beach

Guaymas

Gulf of California

Chihuahua

Divisadero
Barranca del Cobre
(Copper Canyon)

Los Mochis

Monterrey

La Paz

Durango

Mazatlan

Cabo San Lucas

Pacific Ocean

Tepic

Leon
Guanajuato

Guadalajara

Salamanca

Puerto Vallarta

Jurica

Lake Chapala

Tequisquia

Atenquique

Manzanillo

Avandaro

Las Truchas

Taxco

Zihuatanejo

Acapulco